T0274443

Chilies and Chances

Chilies and Chances

Lao Gan Ma

and Her

Spicy

Empire

Wu Hua

Books Beyond Boundaries

ROYAL COLLINS

Chilies and Chances: Lao Gan Ma and Her Spicy Empire

By Wu Hua
Translated by Wu Meilian
Edited by Greg Jones

First published in 2024 by Royal Collins Publishing Group Inc.
Groupe Publication Royal Collins Inc.
550-555 boul. René-Lévesque O Montréal (Québec) H2Z1B1 Canada

10 9 8 7 6 5 4 3 2 1

ISBN: 978-1-4878-1264-5

To find out more about our publications, please visit
www.royalcollins.com.

Contents

Contents

Introduction

Tao Huabi was born in 1947. She entered the chili sauce industry at the age of forty-two and successfully popularized the chili sauce brand Lao Gan Ma all over the world.

Thanks to the reform and opening-up policy, Tao built her chili sauce kingdom and became a legend among entrepreneurs in China and around the world.

After she became one of the "first rich," Tao didn't forget to help others on their way to prosperity. Starting from a small restaurant, her company has grown into an enterprise that pays annual taxes of more than 500 million *yuan*, funds 280 thousand *mu*[*] of pollution-free chili pepper fields in seven counties in Guizhou Province in Southwest China, and directly and indirectly improves the economic wellbeing of almost eight million rural people.

---

[*] One *mu* equals about 0.16 acres.

For more than twenty years, Tao never owed the government a penny, never took a loan, and never earned money that she shouldn't have. People said she was silly, but she didn't agree. She believed that paying taxes was honorable.

"I run my business honestly. I don't steal, and I don't give other people excuses to take me down."

She never owes money to her employees, agents, and suppliers; otherwise, she would be too anxious to sleep. "I don't owe you anything, and you don't owe me anything. I only care about the quality of my products on the market."

Tao insists that her company not be publicly listed. She teaches her son to be a good person and businessman, never invest in shares, make the company a holding company or a listed one, or take loans. She wants her children and grandchildren to continue to make Lao Gan Ma big and prosperous within their capabilities.

"What I do is a real industry. I am honest to my ancestors, the people, and the government," she said.

Tao is an honest person, and she only tells the truth. She hopes her offspring could also be honest people and honest businessmen. "To everyone, being honest is always good," she said.

Even though Lao Gan Ma never advertised its brand, it can be found anywhere around the world where Chinese people live. Lao Gan Ma has truly created a legend of creating and keeping wealth in all economic situations with no financing, no loans, no listing, and no advertisements.

In life, Tao believes in modesty and integrity.

In crises, she believes in staying away from loan financing.

When she started her business, she believed in making it honest and clean.

After realizing her first dream, she believes in going forward and finding her second dream.

When she sees her accomplishment, she believes in maintaining the rules and philosophies that got her there.

While many people focus on Tao's wealth and success, few pay attention to her story of fighting and growth before she became famous.

A Life of Legend

Lao Gan Ma and Tao Huabi

—Chapter One—

The Origin of Tao Huabi's Name

"Lao Gan Ma is wherever Chinese people live." Some people even think Lao Gan Ma is the Coca-Cola of China. Lao Gan Ma became an internationally famous brand like Coca-Cola, but its history is a lot shorter.

But maybe, many years later, Tao Huabi's offspring will build a museum for Lao Gan Ma in Guiyang, as the Coca-Cola company did in Atlanta, to tell the story of Lao Gan Ma and her legendary chili sauce kingdom.

This is what the world expects the company to do, but Lao Gan Ma only has a very simple introduction on its official website, "Lao Gan Ma is a brand created from scratch by the company's founder, Ms. Tao Huabi. In 1996, Tao Huabi founded a factory in Longdongbao, Guiyang, to produce flavored black bean products. After twenty years of development, Lao Gan Ma has become a widely welcomed brand of chili sauce among Chinese people domestically and internationally."

"Created from scratch." With a humble origin, Tao created her own legend and gradually became a model for Chinese entrepreneurs with her forbearance, diligence, integrity, and unremitting efforts.

Stories about Tao depict her as a poor, hardworking, honest, smart, and sassy woman. Her sassiness is what makes her chili sauce unique. These qualities are the best footnotes for understanding the life of Tao, the "superwoman of chili sauce."

Tao was born in Yongxing Township, Meitan County, Zunyi City, Guizhou Province. When the Second Sino-Japanese War broke out in 1937, under the leadership of its president Zhu Kezhen, who was also a renowned geographer, meteorologist, and educator, National Chekiang University (NCKU) moved west and resumed operation in Yongxing from 1940 to June 1946 with the belief of "saving and developing the country with education and science." At that time, a large group of scientists, including Zhu Kezhen, Tan Jiazhen, Su Buqing, Lu Hefu, Wang Ganchang, Bei Shizhang, and Chen Jiangong, gathered here and left a long-lasting impact on the economic and cultural development in the isolated township.

Tao was born in a turbulent time, and she didn't have an opportunity to go to school. However, she grew up in an environment developed by great people, and she was blessed with extraordinary intelligence in management, which she was fully aware of. Once, during an interview, she joked with the host, "I may be old, but my head is no less useful than young people's like yours."

After the war ended in 1945, the professors and students of NCKU began to return to the original school site in Hangzhou in 1946. Tao was born in January 1947, a few months after they left.

It was the time of the War of Liberation or the Second Kuomintang-Communist Civil War.

On that day, the Tao family was busy and happily preparing to welcome the new member.

Rural households in northern Guizhou mostly lived separately from each other but close to their own land. People's lives were highly dependent on the bazaars, where products were mainly transported by manpower and horses. Tao's parents earned their livings by selling fabric at the bazaars, and their home located on flat land with fertile soil. However, poverty, war, and rampant bandits made the region desolate.

The villages at that time had no doctors, only a midwife—a woman with laboring experience—to help. The midwives were well respected for helping all women give birth in many neighboring villages. They were seen as "the goddesses who bring children" and "Boddhisatvas who save lives." Some women survived, but some died. Childbirth was a big event that brought joy and anxiety to all rural families, regardless of rich and poor, given the dangers that awaited the mothers. "The distance between their lives and deaths is as thin as a piece of paper, and they can be lost to the afterworld within one cry."

In the Tao family, the fire was burning hot in the kitchen, and people were busy boiling water, slaughtering chicken, making soup, and passing clothes. It was not Tao's mother's first time giving birth, but the midwife still gave her an egg to make her labor smooth. "Girl, eat this; you'll have strength!" she said. Eggs were the best nutrient. Women ate chicken soup and eggs in sweet wine after giving birth.

Tao's mother was in pain, and her father was distraught. He had to help bring water, cook, and care for his older children. He did not know if his third child would be a son or a daughter and if his wife and his newborn would be safe. He also did not know that this child would become so outstanding when she grew up.

"Mother and child are both fine," said the midwife. "Congratulations, it's an embroiderer!"

The midwives announced the gender of the newborns in a tactful way to protect the pride of the patriarchal families. The "embroiderers" or "stove workers" were girls, and "shepherds" and "runners on the hills" were boys.

Rural families valued their lineages very much. "Married daughters were like spilled water," and "they follow their husbands, regardless of who they are or what they do." Daughters belonged to their husbands' families after they married, and only sons could carry on the family line.

But Tao Huabi's arrival was a happy surprise to the Tao family, who already had two sons. But the father soon felt anxious again because the family was already struggling financially.

Rural families preferred to give their children ugly names, like Maodan, Goudan, Choudan, and Lüdan for boys or Dani and Erni for girls. They believed children with ugly names were not attractive to ghosts and demons that could take them away from this world and thus could grow up safe and sound. This was largely related to the poor living conditions and the lack of medications. People were terrified by the raging illnesses.

The old people in the village named the baby girl Chunmei, "spring plum blossom," hoping she could have a beautiful life like the flowers in spring.

The Tao house was surrounded by mountains covered with pine forests. The trees howled as the wind blew past them. People said this was the voice of the mountain god. Little Tao was both attracted to and terrified of the forest, not knowing what was hiding in the dark.

When she grew older, Tao and her brothers went to the forest, and they found a small piece of land behind it decorated with wildflowers. It became the kids' secret playground.

In the 1950s, to meet the needs of production and construction in China, many pine trees had to be cut down for timber. People often came to Tao's hometown for the trees. At that time, local transportation was not convenient, and it was difficult to move the trees after they were cut down. Sometimes, the trunks had to be sawn into pieces, leaving the branches in the villages for firewood.

The land near Tao's home was flat and fertile, capable of producing grain. After the founding of the People's Republic of China, people's communes were established here, which later developed into farms. Everyone with certain working abilities had to work and earn "work points" in exchange for food. The people's communes were the basic unit of Chinese society, combining workers, farmers, businesses, students, and military members.

The isolated village became lively with the visiting strangers from other townships and provinces. They spoke differently, and they sang work songs when they sawed and carried timber.

One day, two men, one young and one old, with strange accents, came to the village. Tao thought they were like other strangers who would leave after they cut the trees. But this time was different. Adults said the two men would stay, and they would poison and kidnap the children. Thus, all the village children looked at the two strangers with fear.

They looked around the village and started to find hoes to level an open space at the village entrance. They cut off the dense roots and removed weeds. In an afternoon's time, a square piece of land with a yellow mud bottom was cleared out.

Then, the two men borrowed wall panels and began to build walls. After ten days, the walls were already as tall as a person.

Building a house was a big event involving multiple rituals in the rural area. The owners had to select the location and date, cut trees, invite carpenters, build the frame, build the roof, install the gate, and settle the tablets for gods and ancestors.

People believed the location of the house was important to the *fengshui* of the household and determined the family's fortune. A *fengshui* master needed to first choose the location and then the auspicious date for construction. The other procedures also needed to consider the time. Finally, a grand ceremony would be held upon the completion of the house, and the master engineer would give his blessings.

However, these two out-of-towners did not go through any of these rituals. Tao watched them every day, and she saw that they simply built the house frame with some trees and used plastic sheeting to cover the windows without any scruple to the dates. Then, they built a bed and a stove and added some furniture. They worked hard. As soon as they were finished with the house, they went to find firewood in the mountains and grew vegetables by the house.

When her older brothers went to work in the mountains, Tao followed them to collect wild herbs and pinecones. They would deliberately get around the strangers' mysterious new house, fearing being kidnapped. Some naughty children would shout "out-of-towners!" as a joke and scare little ones like Tao to run.

But the two "out-of-towners" were competent workers. In just a few months, they filled their front and back yards with big

firewood piles, leaving the kids responsible for collecting firewood watching. Some teenagers began to steal this firewood, but
the two men never stopped them. After that, they began to steal
the vegetables, too.

Stealing was a serious crime in the village. Once, when Tao
saw the village children stealing the vegetables from the men,
she suddenly became indignant and felt unjust for them. She
screamed at the top of her lungs, "Thief! Thief!" and ran to the
house to report to the owners.

She expected the "out-of-towners" to be angry, but the older
man smiled and said, "It's ok. They're just kids. We don't blame
them."

Tao did not understand. Then she asked, "Will you poison
us? Will you kidnap children for money?"

"No! No!" answered the man, laughing.

He assured the little girl that he and his friend were good
people and then handed her a cooked sweet potato. Tao was
afraid, "What if he was a bad guy? What if he had infectious
disease?"

But she could not resist the rare delicacy in front of her. Her
family had only wild herbs for food. The old man patted her on
her head and said, "Don't be afraid, child. It's not poisonous."

Tao looked at him for a minute and accepted the sweet potato. She gorged it down. "Easy, easy, child. I will give you more," said the man. He then told her stories about his past, when he was a soldier fighting for his country to be free.

The man became Tao's first teacher; even though he never gave her an official class as in school, he opened her eyes to a world she had never heard of. She learned about the brave little pony who finally crossed the river by itself, the indomitable old man who was determined to dig through the great mountain blocking his house, and the many martyrs and revolutionary pioneers who sacrificed themselves for a better future. The old man later gave Tao a new name: Huabi—*hua* for China, and *bi* for glory.

Since then, little Tao Huabi began to dream about the outside world with trains, cars, and skyscrapers.

Tao Huabi's Life-Long Mentor

Tao Huabi never knew the old man's name. She only knew that he was a college student and had learned a lot of life skills when the NCKU moved west. In her eyes, the old man was a kind, educated, and talented person.

One day, when she visited him as usual, the old man said, "Child, I'll make you a pair of cloth shoes."

"Cloth shoes!" Tao was shocked. She had never had a pair of cloth shoes, nor had she seen the old man himself wearing a pair, only straw sandals. She thought he was just joking, so she said, "Grandpa, you should make a pair for yourself. I don't need them." She couldn't imagine how he could make a pair of shoes for her when he had nothing to wear.

Many people in the village wore straw sandals, and the poor had to go barefoot. Tao's mother had a pair of cloth shoes, but she only wore them on the New Year and when visiting friends. The man took out a piece of old bedsheet and some clothes for the shoes. Then, he cut out the shape of Tao's feet on bamboo coats.

Tao had seen her mother making shoes. She had to make the sole, cut the top and sides, and spin the thread.

It took a lot of time and effort to make shoes. The old man glued layers of fabric together and let them dry. Then, he cut them into the shape of shoe soles. After that, he began to reinforce the soles with thread on a big needle.

After ten days or so, the old man put the new shoes in front of Tao. The girl felt she could fly up to the sky when she held the shoes in her hands.

But before she could enjoy her precious gift, the Great Famine struck. Up until this day, Tao clearly remembered the horror of hunger when she dreamed of putting mud in her mouth just to feel full. She hated to see people waste food since then, and she made "do not waste food" the strictest rule in her company's dining hall.

Food soon ran out, first the grain, then the potatoes, then the radish. Wild herbs that were used to feed the pigs became life saviors. People cooked the herbs in water, added some cornmeal and salt if they had it, and served to the whole family. Children, old people, and sick people who could not digest such meals grew weaker and weaker day by day before they died of starvation.

People who have suffered from long-term starvation became too weak to walk. Tao couldn't visit the old man for a long time because her strength could only support her finding wild herbs with her family. She watched her parents cook and immediately reached out for the food when it was done.

One day, she felt she was stronger than usual, so she went to visit the old man, only to find him on the verge of death. The younger man had already left, and the old man could not survive the winter.

Soon after that, the old man passed away. He told Tao that she must always be diligent and honest and never brag or lie. Lies were the cause of the famine.

Tao could not yet understand that, but she learned that lies would lead to trouble.

The old man's words were engraved in Tao's heart and continued to influence her throughout her life.

An Outstanding Skill

People learn best from experiences, both their own and other people's. After the famine, Tao experimented with different cooking methods to make meals delicious for her family. Zunyi is rich in chili peppers and its byproducts, such as fried chili peppers and pickled peppers. Tao often made appetizers with chili pepper herself, which greatly improved the flavor of bland food at home.

Chili peppers are inevitable in Guizhou people's lives, especially when supplies are scarce. People believe that chili peppers can ward off evil spirits. For example, they would make a chili pepper with red cloth for children if they do not stop crying; put three chili peppers on top of the soybean milk when making tofu; shoot a chili pepper away on an arrow to cure backache.

In *The Book of Qian*, it is recorded, "Due to the lack of salt, [people in Guizhou] used chili peppers instead, to replace saltiness with spiciness." The *Sizhoufu Gazetteer* also records chili peppers as a type of medicine, "Sea pepper, also called spicy fire. The locals use it to replace salt."[*]

People in Guizhou plant cabbage in winter and chili peppers in spring. After the chili peppers are harvested in summer, the land is ready for planting cabbage again. All Guizhou rural families know how to make chili pepper sauce with red peppers and some local spices. Tao learned it when she was young, and her sauce was quite famous in her community. She was very devoted to making food, and her sauce was a lot spicier and crunchier than others.

Many people asked her about her secret, and she always said, "There's nothing special about my sauce; I just pay more attention to the fire when cooking it." She never considered herself superior or special in any way. All she did was not miss

---

[*] *The Book of Qian* (黔书 *qián shū*) and *Sizhoufu Gazetteer* (思州府志 *sī zhōu fǔ zhi*) are both Guizhou local chronicles from the 17th century.

any ingredient, put enough amount of each, and pay full attention to the fire. She didn't know how far her skill of making chili sauce would take her.

Leaving Home

In the mid-1960s, Tao was an adult working both at home and in the community. During the day, she worked with other people in the field, and she cooked meals for her family when she returned home. Hard living made her diligent and determined.

As an important part of the "Learn from Dazhai in Agriculture" campaign,[*] water conservancy construction had shifted from focusing on flood control in the past to comprehensive development and utilization. To actively respond to Chairman Mao's call that "water conservancy is the lifeblood of agriculture," water conservancy construction focusing on solving agricultural water conservancy and drought relief problems was built everywhere, including Yongxing Township.

---

[*] The "Learn from Dazhai in Agriculture" campaign was organized by Mao Zedong in 1963. The campaign encouraged peasants from all over China to follow the example of the farmers of the village Dazhai in Shanxi by practicing self-reliance in rural development.

Tao participated in the construction, carrying soil and rocks with the other workers.

There was a man from Guiyang in the village at that time, and he taught Tao a lot of things.

He told her about Lei Feng's (a model worker and soldier) stories and his spirit of selflessly serving the country and the people. He also told her about his own stories of fighting against the Japanese army and creating a better life for the Chinese people.

He also told her what the "pillars of the nation" were. The pillars supporting a house need to be upright, and the pillars supporting a nation need to be honest and responsible. As long as everyone united together, they could build their country prosperous, he said.

Tao didn't know how to be a pillar of the nation, but she felt motivated by the man's words. They made her feel hopeful about the future.

The man died, but his wish of planting fir trees was unfinished. Tao watered all the sprouts he brought and planted them all the next spring after he died. She could see his aspiration in every one of them.

Then, Tao decided to find the man's family. They must be waiting for him at home, and they should know where he was during his last days and where to find his grave.

Tao didn't tell anyone about her plan. Her family would think she was mad to think of traveling to another city for a complete stranger, and the production team wouldn't allow her to leave the village either. So, she just left on her own with some of the man's belongings.

However, when she arrived at Guiyang, she could not find the man's family at all. Finally, she found the place where he worked, but no one there knew him.

Seeing her waiting at the gate every day, the gatekeeper asked her what she wanted, so Tao told him about the man's story. The gatekeeper was deeply touched but told her the man had probably stopped working there long ago.

The gatekeeper then suggested Tao work at a nursing home so that she could support herself in this strange city. "You are a kind, honest girl; that's why I recommended you to them," he said.

With no other choice, Tao accepted the job. The job was dirty, heavy, and exhaustive, but she persisted despite all the hardship, remembering the stories of all the great people she had heard. She had a place to stay and food to eat.

The Beginning of Her Business

Achieving
"Cold Boot"

—Chapter Two—

How to Begin a Business without Money?

Working at the nursing home was hard, both physically and mentally. Tao was often yelled at for minor errors, but she never complained. To her, nothing could compare with the starving days she had experienced when she was young. They trained her to be hardworking, forbearing, and resilient.

An older woman liked Tao and introduced her to Li. Li was the accountant of the 206 Geological Team of the Ministry of Nuclear Industry. He was young, educated, and with a stable and well-paid job.

The two young people liked each other, and they soon got married.

After she had her first child, Tao quit her job at the nursing home. A few years later, China ushered in reform and opening-up period.

Reform and opening-up was a policy that China began to implement domestic reform and opening to the outside world after the Third Plenary Session of the Eleventh Central Committee of the Communist Party of China in December 1978. China's domestic reform first started in rural areas. In November 1978, Xiaogang Village in Fengyang County, Anhui Province, implemented the household contract responsibility system of "dividing farmland to each household and taking responsibility for its own profits and losses," which kicked off China's domestic reform. In cities, the management rights of state-owned enterprises have been significantly improved.

Tao noticed the changes around her with excitement. She didn't yet realize how these changes would influence her own life and how she was about to change China's private economy in the future.

The 1980s was a time of cultural reconstruction in China. Intellectuals were keen to talk about humanitarianism, democracy, equality, and the rule of law. People had the opportunity to rediscover their individualities and values. Tao was one of them, and she developed hopeful plans. This may be considered the first step to her success.

The reform and opening-up was the second significant revolution in China. In over forty years, China has made great achievements in development, and its people's lives have been highly improved from poverty to moderate prosperity.

Since then, trading was no longer forbidden. More and more people around Tao began to do small businesses. Then, the "Down to the Countryside Movement"* stopped, and students returned to the cities. These were because the Third Plenary Session of the Eleventh Central Committee proposed developing a collective ownership economy and solving the problems of urban labor and employment.

In 1980, the central government convened a national conference on labor and employment and further proposed the policy that "under the overall planning and guidance of the state, the labor department shall implement employment introduction, voluntary organized employment, and self-employment." It pointed out that the individual economy of urban workers had initially recovered and developed, but it could not meet the needs of national economic development. Policies must be further adjusted to be widely and deeply publicized.

The radio promoted the important role of the individual economy of urban workers in developing production, revitalizing the economy, meeting needs, and expanding employment. The individual economy of urban workers should be allowed to develop healthily.

---

* "Down to the Countryside Movement," a campaign launched by Mao Zedong that asked urban youth to experience life by working in rural areas between the mid-1950s and 1978.

In 1981, the Central Committee and the State Council issued Several Decisions on Broadening Open Roads, Revitalizing the Economy, and Solving Urban Employment Issues, and the State Council issued Several Policy Regulations on the Non-Agricultural Individual Economy in Urban Areas. It stipulated that self-employed households were generally operated by one person or a family; when necessary, with the approval of the industrial and commercial administrative department, one or two helpers could be hired; those with strong technical skills or special skills could bring three and no more than five apprentices. Self-employed households were allowed to adopt business methods such as processing of supplied materials, self-production, sales, distribution, and consignment, setting up stalls, selling in streets and alleys, and mobile sales.

The introduction of these policies meant that business was encouraged and protected. Like most Chinese people, Tao had had enough of the cold and starving days. Goods were available only on a coupon basis, and many were often out of stock. Every household lived on coarse grains, cabbage soup, and chili peppers. They only had meat on the New Year's Eve.

More and more booths appeared on the narrow streets of Guiyang, and the callings of their owners for vegetables, fried bread, fruits, and small commodities made the city lively. Tao felt her community suddenly bloom again like a withering flower.

She wanted to start a business, too, but she had no money for that. Later, she and some of her friends decided to be vegetable retailers. They bought vegetables in bulk from farmers at wholesale prices and sold them at retail prices to earn the price difference. It was a lot harder than it sounds.

At first, Tao restocked from places like Maoshajing and Tangbaguan that were near the city, but then she realized that the farmers in those regions were aware of the retail prices in Guiyang and would not give her a favorable price. Therefore, she decided to go restock in farther places like Huaxi and Longdongbao for more money.

To do that, she and her friends needed to leave home at 3:00 a.m., walk for 20–30 kilometers with a torch, and return with the vegetables on foot. They tried to arrive at the selling spots before breakfast; otherwise, it would take a whole day to sell everything.

It was not very heavy work, but it was tiring. Some neighbors wanted to join Tao and her team but quickly quit because of exhaustion. Tao did not have other commitments at the time, and she was satisfied with what she could earn from this job.

Tao's husband had an urban household registration but no property. After their child was born, the couple's biggest wish was to build their own house. Her husband's salary could only support the family's basic expenses, so Tao worked hard to save money. When she saw her child's lovely face, she forgot all her weariness. She firmly held on to her dream of buying a new house, which she believed stood for a bright future for her family. She would do anything to make this dream come true. Whenever she came across challenges with her business, she thought about the stories of the revolutionary pioneers to motivate herself.

After a few years, Tao saved up about 10,000 *yuan*, which was a considerable amount. She began looking for places to build a house and calculating expenses for construction and building materials. She was comparing prices of different brands of doors and windows, even small things like wires and light bulbs.

Then, her second son was born. Many times, in her dream, she saw her family living happily in a big, bright home with a new bed, sofa, and stove. Her children are running and laughing.

One day, when her husband returned home from work, Tao talked about her plans for the new house. He, on the other hand, did not show enthusiasm as he always did. "What's wrong?" she asked. "I don't know, just tired. Maybe I'm sick," he answered.

"Maybe, but don't worry. We'll go to the hospital tomorrow. Whatever it is, the doctors will definitely find the cure for you." Her husband nodded and went to sleep.

The next day, the couple went to the hospital. "Maybe you're just too tired recently. There's probably nothing serious," Tao said after a whole day's examination.

Her husband sighed, "Hope so." A few days later, the hospital told them to go again.

Tao's husband was diagnosed with emphysema. The news was disastrous to the family. It meant that Tao's husband would become a frequent visitor to the hospital and that their dream of buying a new house had broken.

One day, with tears in his eyes, Tao's husband asked Tao to stop spending money on his treatment and save it for their children. But how could Tao give up her beloved husband and the father of her sons? She told him that she would do anything to cure him, and the family must move on together.

Tao's life became harder with two children and a sick husband to support at home. She left early every day to sell the vegetables. Sometimes, she could sell them within a few hours, but sometimes, it took longer. Her elder son would then watch over the booth, and Tao would quickly eat and see how her husband was doing. Her husband was sorry to see her languish, but she assured him that she was fine.

With no medical insurance, the family's money soon ran out, but her husband did not get better. Tao began to increase her workload and extend her working hours. Sometimes, her children would bring her food to the booth, and she would eat it with her chili sauce. Her children were often attracted by the delicious smell of the sauce and wanted to try it.

While she could keep her children entertained, she could not help her husband. She did not have any more money to pay for his treatment, but she also could not bear to give up. Tao thus borrowed a loan, the first loan in her life, a usurious loan.

One day, her husband wanted to eat some meat, so Tao bought some with all her money. She made some meatballs, and the long-lost smell of meat filled the room.

When she brought the meatballs to her husband, the two children couldn't stop staring and swallowing. Tao didn't want their father to see it, so she told them to go out and play.

The father looked at the bowl, his eyes filled with tears. Tao said, "Don't mind them. They'll have plenty to eat when they grow up. You need this now to get better. When you get better, go make money and buy them everything they want!"

He listened and wiped his eyes. "Take good care of our sons," he said, "I will not be able to see them grow to be men." His words broke Tao's heart. She knew his illness was serious, but she always believed that he would get better. He did not.

Tao's husband died in 1984. When the news came, Tao felt blood rush to her head, and tears streamed down her face. She fell to the floor, stiff and cold, and could not say a word.

How to Pay Back the Debt?

Tao was left alone with two young children, a huge debt, and endless sorrow. Fortunately, the Geological Team subsidized her family 30 *yuan* every month, which solved many of her urgent needs.

Many people wanted Tao to date and find a new husband, but she always refused. She promised her husband she would take good care of their sons, so she could not take the risk of finding someone who did not love them. Whenever someone came for this purpose, she would say, "Wait until my boys are married." Slowly, those people stopped coming.

Sometime later, Tao went to Guangdong for better work opportunities. She took a lot of chili sauce with her to have some familiar taste in an unfamiliar province and to save money on eating.

As early as July 15, 1979, the central government officially approved Guangdong and Fujian provinces to implement special policies and flexible measures in foreign economic activities. The South has implemented reform and opening-up, and many factories have sprung up. While in Guangdong, Tao wondered if she could open a factory in Guiyang. But she knew that this was impossible. She didn't even know if she could pay off the debt she owed.

Tao's chili sauce was widely welcomed among her coworkers in Guangdong, but she had never thought of turning it into a business. All she thought about was paying off her debt, and she sent money back as soon as she received her salary. Her heart was with her children in Guiyang, but she could neither write nor call. Finally, she decided not to separate from them and returned home.

Hearing about the news, Tao's sons, Li Guishan and Li Hui, waited for her at the village gate days before her return. They would sit there every day until dark and until some adults brought them home.

Tao began selling vegetables again. Her straw sandals often got ruined in the rain, and she had to walk barefoot on the cinder road. Her feet were bruised, bled, and then scuffed again after it had healed.

Fortunately, her children helped her considerably during this time, especially Guishan, who helped her watch the booth. Many people bought vegetables from Tao's booth, and they often gave more money than they should.

When she could not sell everything at the booth in time, Tao had to walk around the streets trying to sell the rest. Her whole body, especially the right shoulder, would ache and sore terribly afterward, but she had to rise again after four to five hours of sleep to restock for the next day.

Although she had tried all she could to earn and save money, Tao could only save several *yuan* every day, but the interest on her loan kept growing until it reached several thousand *yuan*. Tao was desperate. She could never pay back her debt in this way. Therefore, she took another job of helping people carry rocks. After she finished selling vegetables, she went to carry rocks on the hills until midnight. Soon after she lay down, she needed to get up again to restock vegetables. The pain in her feet when walking became less and less acute as the calluses on her soles grew thicker and thicker. Many times, she would almost fall asleep by the road after carrying the rocks. People were all surprised to see her losing so much weight all of a sudden and asked, "What happened? You are almost a skeleton now!"

Tao answered, "That's fate. I'm born a laboring person; I just can't put on any weight."

Her debt almost killed her, but she managed to pay it all off. Since then, she constantly warned herself and her sons, "Never take loans, and try not to borrow money from others either. Use whatever you have, whether much or little, always use your own money."

Differentiated Operations in the Snack Industry

Seeing the profit in the vegetable market, more and more people joined in and intensified the competition. The booth owners often had to fight for a spot on the street.

Some vendors used lighter scales to attract more customers, pretending to offer a cheaper price than others by giving less amount. They also advised Tao to do the same, but she insisted on being honest with her business because she knew cheating was not the way to achieve long-term success.

However, Tao also realized that she could not stay in the vegetable business anymore if she wanted to keep earning money, so she decided to start another business. After evaluating the situation in her surrounding neighborhood and excluding some existing options like fruit shops, tofu shops, and department stores, Tao chose to sell starch jelly and rice tofu.

She may not be able to elaborate on her reasons for this decision, but growing up in poverty and having experienced great time changes, her instincts and ability to spot and seize opportunities told her that she made the right choice.

Her shop stood out among all the neighboring shops. Her products were ready-made and served cold, which saved her many troubles during the selling. This small success was already a reflection of Tao's outstanding business acumen.

The Supplier Thinking of a Small Stall Owner

Tao, at this time, began to develop a business leadership mindset.

During the early marketization process, counterfeiting and missing parts and quantity were very common. But Tao never used these tactics. Her determination to earn every penny cleanly made her future success destined.

Tao's starch jelly and rice tofu were cheap, delicious, and large in portion. She stuck fast to her business philosophy, "good quality at an affordable price." It was a popular phrase at the time, but few people could do it.

Tao also had her special customers. Many people who sold candies and popcorn liked to hang around residential areas, but Tao knew she would have better sales near schools, where many students liked to buy her snacks on their way home.

At this time in Guiyang, being a self-employed trader was a popular job. While wages in national enterprises and institutions remained at a low level before the reform, "Tea eggs bring more money than atomic bombs," meaning that people who engaged in high-technology jobs did not earn as much as those who did small businesses. As a result, many people gave up their "iron rice bowl" and became mutton skewers.

Every night, Tao would stay up late to cook the starch jelly and rice tofu. In the morning, while the snacks were cooling, Tao went to buy new ingredients. After she got home, she went selling at a booth near the 206 Geological Team station. She chose this location because she had a large customer population there: teachers and students at the Guizhou Police College, staff members of the Geological Team, and neighbors and acquaintances from home.

In addition to selling at her own booth, Tao also had "supplier thinking" and wholesale some of her products to other stalls. She often visited other traders and chatted with them to know their needs. She would also give advice to booth owners who had difficulties making and selling starch jellies. Later, when those owners realized how good Tao's jellies were, they agreed to purchase from her booth for their own. Tao always gave them a favorable price. Finally, her starch jelly and rice tofu became quite well-known in the area.

Making Rice Tofu the Best Seller

Tao's children could now help her with many things. Together, they built a shed for selling starch jelly so that Tao did not have to carry the snacks to the streets. Slowly, they added a waterproof roof and tables and chairs to it so that people could sit down and eat.

Her sons, Guishan and Hui, helped her carry the heavy items and watch the booth every day. Tao sometimes wanted them to rest, but they said, "Mom, we are big boys now. People will laugh at us if you do not let us work." Tao was very happy to see them so energetic and supportive.

Back then, when telephones were not yet popular, the children played an essential role in passing information and goods between Tao and other traders.

Born in the "land of chili peppers," Tao was an expert in cooking oily chili peppers. She knew how to choose the best materials and how to make the product spicy and crispy, suitable for eating with any staple food. After using Tao's ingredients, the businesses of some struggling stores greatly improved.

One day, Tao had a high fever and could not cook the oily chili peppers for the next day, so she asked her sons to buy some from another store and to watch the booth for the morning. As soon as she arrived at the booth that afternoon, some old customers came to complain about that day's oily peppers. "It's not good at all. What happened to your usual chili peppers?" they asked. Tao explained to them and stayed up late that night to cook more oily peppers for the next day.

Although these were just the spice to the snacks, her customers loved the oily peppers, and some even asked to bring some back home. Tao felt like a proud poet who received acknowledgment for her work—to hear positive comments on her food was her greatest dream. Later, she put an extra bowl of oily chili peppers next to her booth for customers who wanted to take some back.

Unlike many businessmen who purely pursued profit, Tao remained highly alert to capital and her own avarice from the very beginning. Even now, when the calls for corporate financialization and the capitalization of her chili pepper sauce empire have grown louder than ever, Tao always firmly refuses to financialize and capitalize her chili peppers like everything else with potential profits in the marketplace, such as liquor, tea, and big data.

Her business has gone beyond the mainstream of simple profit-seeking and was even a little idealistic. All she had hoped for was that her cuisine would be recognized by the society around her. This goal allowed her to stay focused when dealing with the madding crowd in the business world and to find her unique path to success.

Slowly, oily chili peppers became Tao's secret weapon that made her starch jellies and rice tofu stand out. For years, she concentrated on how to make her oily chili peppers more delicious, and her skills, without doubt, perfected even more.

The Way of a Great Business

To Benefit One's Self and Others

−Chapter Three−

An Economical Consumption Experience

T he steady growth in her starch jelly and rice tofu sales relieved Tao's financial burden. She fully devoted herself to her business, buying materials, cooking, processing, delivering, and selling at the stall. Soon, she realized that her oily chili peppers were particularly popular with diners, and some even came to eat starch jelly and rice tofu just for the chili.

In the 1990s, Chinese brands began to truly enter the arena of rules and differentiation. With the help of others, Tao opened a restaurant near the school of Longdongbao in 1989. The name of her restaurant was *Shihui*, "economical," which explicitly showed Tao's positioning: delicious and affordable. However, Tao had not yet made oily chili peppers her focus because she only considered them a kind of spice, not a real cuisine.

Shihui Restaurant was a shed built with bricks, rocks, and asbestos tiles by Tao and her children. Leaning on the wall of Guizhou Police College, the restaurant had better tables, chairs, and covers than her previous starch jelly stall. The cheap snacks in large portions attracted many middle school students nearby.

Tao always made her restaurant clean for her customers. She welcomed them with a smile and addressed their needs promptly. If she had too much work at hand, she told her guests to help themselves and take whatever spices they needed. When she had time, she chatted and joked with them.

Tao also customized her service for different guests. For truck drivers who came after a long-distance trip, she offered them big bowls so that they could quickly recover their strength. For female students, she offered smaller portions, and for boys, she gave more jelly.

Before long, Shihui Restaurant became many people's favorite for the economical consumption experience it provided. As it grew bigger, Tao could afford to pay some students to help her with the work, and the students also invited their teachers to dine in the restaurant.

Tao kept her interest low because she believed in "small profit and quick return." Tao charged only for the starch jelly but never for her oily chili. As more and more customers requested some oily chili, Tao prepared jars for the take-outs. Guiyang people often said, "The closer you are with your customers, the better your business will be." Tao treated her customers as friends, and she felt hopeful about this new business.

Many of her customers were students from struggling families. Their parents tried all they could to send them to study in Guiyang, hoping they could have better life options than being farmers. Born in a poor family herself, Tao understood these young people's difficulties just by looking at their clothes and the way they paid. Therefore, she paid special attention to these students when they came by giving them more food, asking them where they came from, how their studies were going, where they planned on going after graduation, etc.

Tao, at this time, was not the inexperienced housewife who sold vegetables by the street anymore. She knew how to fight back in life when needed. After she returned from the city with full baskets of raw materials, bus drivers would often refuse to let her ride in public transportation. Tao would not let them mistreat her without yelling back for their discrimination. She dreamed of having a car because she knew she must be strong enough to support her two children.

Even though she had never attended school, Tao learned a lot from life and business: the cost of cheating would eventually fall upon the one who cheats. Doing business was like winning a soccer match, which required time, strength, stamina, and explosive power. Therefore, Tao bet her whole life's time—even her children's—for this game, and she began to make a name for herself in Guiyang's catering business. In a time of profit-seeking and fraud, Tao created a legend with integrity and unconventional delicacy.

A "Unconventional" Businessman's Way of Doing Business

Tao was hot-tempered, but she had a warm, gentle soul. She often chatted with the students who dined and helped out in her restaurant, taking care of them and telling them what was good and what was bad.

Among the children, there was a small, smart girl nicknamed "Peter Pan." Once, after she had helped Tao clean the restaurant, the girl asked if she could bring an extra bowl of starch jelly to her roommate. Tao agreed, so the girl put some leftover jelly into a bowl. Then, Tao looked up and said, "Take more if that's not enough."

"Peter Pan" blushed, thinking she was being sarcastic. But Tao smiled and added, "You kids are young. You can't starve yourselves when your bodies are growing."

Later, Tao learned that "Peter Pan's" roommate was from the countryside and often did not have money to buy dinner.

Hearing this, Tao's own memory of starving rushed back to her, and all she could think of was how to help those poor students in ways their parents far away would hope and in ways she hoped her own sons Guishan and Hui could receive when they were far away from her. Therefore, while all other restaurants had forbidden students to dine on credit, Tao always allowed them when they did not have enough money. For those who could only afford half the portion, she gave them in full.

Ouyang was a frequent customer of Tao's. He was a naughty student at a technical school nearby. When he first came to the Shihui Restaurant, he was wiping sweat off his face with his T-shirt while calling, "One vegetarian jelly, with extra jelly!" like a young unruly hero from the classic novel *Water Margin*. Other customers told Tao that he was a troublemaker who often involved himself in fighting and violence.

Ouyang ate a lot, and he never had trouble paying. Then, for some time, he only ordered vegetarian jellies. When asked, he admitted with embarrassment, "I'm a little tight lately."

"Don't starve yourself! You need the nutrition," said Tao, adding extra jelly for him for free. "Work hard on your studies and get a good job," she continued as usual, "Don't live a hard life like me."

Ouyang said, "You're the only one in Guiyang who cares about me. I'll do what you say."

One day, Ouyang came again during class time. Tao was very angry, as if it was her own son who skipped class. She shouted at the boy, "Did your parents send you to the city for this? They are working in the field to pay for your school, and what are you doing here? How can you ever face them again if you fail to graduate?"

Ouyang did not answer. He quickly finished eating and apologized to Tao, "Aunt Tao, I'm sorry. I'll go to school right now."

After that, Ouyang never came to the restaurant. Tao did not pay much attention to it until one day, she heard Ouyang was planning to return home due to financial problems. Tao immediately called Ouyang to her restaurant. As the boy prepared himself to hear her ask for the money he owed, Tao said, "How can you quit school? Come help me in the restaurant when you have time, and I'll lend you money to finish school. You don't owe me anything. You're like my son."

Hearing this, the boy dropped to his knees and cried, "Aunt Tao, you will be my *laoganma* from today!"

In Guizhou, parents often find their children a *laogandie* (old godfather) or a *laoganma* (old godmother) to bless them with a long, healthy life. Many customers witnessed the touching scene that day, and so everyone began to call Tao *laoganma* since then, workers, students, farmers, truck drivers, and even old people. Slowly, her own name was almost forgotten, and the heart-warming title, *laoganma*, had replaced it and became Tao's special business totem.

Trouble with the Urban Management Department

Every day at 3:00 a.m., Tao had to go to the city several kilometers away from home to restock. She was friends with all the sellers, and they always kept the best vegetables for her. Before returning, she would shop for an hour or two, buying all the needed ingredients.

Getting a bus ride was always difficult, with a huge basket on her back. Some considerate conductors would let her in, but some would not, even when she offered twice the fare. Tao would argue with them, saying she would not get off and trying to stay on the bus longer. But sometimes, the conductors would push her down, and she had to walk all the way back. Her back and shoulders were often frayed and bruised by the heavy basket, not to mention her feet from walking two hours without rest. Therefore, she felt extremely grateful every time she was allowed to ride the bus.

When she returned to her restaurant, she had to start preparing the ingredients to open for customers at seven immediately. Her restaurant closed around ten at night. After that, Tao would start making oily chili peppers, fermented soybeans, and fermented bean curd for the next day. She took every processing step seriously for the best flavor.

By the 1990s, Guizhou responded to the call for reform and opening-up and began to vigorously develop the private economy, lifting all restrictions on the proportion, scale, form, and developmental speed of private enterprises. *Laoganma* Tao's time had come. Her restaurant did not have an advantageous location, delicate decorations, or promotion skills, but everyone knew it, and everyone liked to come for its delicious and authentic taste. Some restaurants liked to shout slogans at the door and even pull customers from the streets, but their sales still could not compete with Tao's. Slowly, seeing the contrasts between themselves and Tao, some jealous restaurant owners came looking for trouble, either blaming Tao for taking away their customers or complaining about the truck drivers who parked their vehicles in front of their doors to dine at Tao's restaurant. Tao bravely confronted and reasoned with them, even when they threatened to fight.

But her trouble did not stop there. Even the urban management department frequently came trying to find faults and reasons to fine. They thought the single mom was an easy target, but they were wrong. Once, a management staff came to her restaurant on the weekend to "fine" her without wearing his uniform or carrying any documentation. "What kind of enforcement is this?" asked Tao, "Everything I do is legal. I pay my taxes, and I'm supported by the government. If you think you can just charge me for whatever reason you come up with, then you can't be more wrong!" Tao knew that if she submitted to it once, she would always be troubled by this matter.

This was the "broken windows theory" raised by James Wilson and George Kelling, who said, "If a window in a building is broken and is left unrepaired, all the rest of the windows will soon be broken." Tao did not know this theory, but she understood compromising would lead to more trouble and would eventually ruin her business. At first, students who helped at her restaurant were all worried that her toughness would offend others, but Tao was not afraid because she did not do anything wrong. "I'm not afraid of other competitors, not even bandits. If they want to kill me, I'll kill them, too!" That is the rule of the jungle and the market: only the powerful survive.

Finding Another Way Out

Tao's secret to running her restaurant was to make the dining experiences satisfying and affordable for her customers. She gave out oily chili peppers for free to those who dined in her restaurant. When such requests increased, she placed ready-made peppers on a stand outside. People who wanted some could take it by themselves and leave the money in a box.

One day, Tao fell ill and did not prepare the peppers. Thinking that one day's deficiency would not influence the restaurant's business, she was surprised to see an unprecedented few customers that day. Tao visited some other restaurants and noticed their businesses were fine, thanks to the peppers they had bought from Tao previously. When she returned, Tao decided to control her sales of oily chili peppers so that other sellers would not take advantage of her skills and her work, which she spent several hours every night to complete.

Despite the exhaustion, Tao noticed that selling oily chili peppers alone was more profitable than everything else in her restaurant combined. Many people came buying the peppers in bowls and pots for daily consumption, and her customer group expanded, too. Many vehicle owners began to come for her products, which was quite an achievement at that time.

The restaurant owner next to hers, the shrewd Mr. Huang, often came to visit. One day, he joked, "What a great sale you have today! There must be several hundred in that box, isn't it? What if someone takes it?"

Tao joked back, "Let him try it. I'll kick his ass!"

People started to tell Tao that she should open a factory to produce her oily chili peppers. Huang heard about it and opened a booth in front of his restaurant to sell oily chili peppers, too. However, he could not compete against Tao at all. People soon stopped buying from him, even when Tao had sold out hers. Sometimes, customers who had already decided to buy Huang's peppers would immediately turn to Tao when she brought out her peppers.

Some students made a bulletin board for Tao's booth with the words "Lao Gan Ma" on it. After that, the name Lao Gan Ma became synonymous with the best chili peppers in town.

Many people came for her reputation, and some in other cities even asked friends in Longdongbao to buy them Lao Gan Ma's oily chili peppers. No media publicized for Tao. People knew her for her for her high-quality product and sincere attitude. Unlike many other business owners, Tao kept her profit on each sale low and never overcharged anyone.

Tao's business welcomed another major increase around 1994 after the highway construction near Longdongbao. She thus redecorated the Shihui Restaurant, hoping her business could keep improving. However, things never went as smoothly as people hoped. As Tao increased her time cooking the chili peppers, some school leaders came to report the influence of the excessive smell of peppers on students' health. Tao thus faced a huge dilemma of leaving her newly renovated restaurant or stopping the chili pepper business that had laid the foundation for her success.

A Humble New Start

Again, people persuaded Tao to give up her restaurant and focus on the chili pepper business. Tao was reluctant to accept this idea because she worried that the poor students would not have affordable meals anymore. "Don't be silly," said the other restaurant owners, "you can open a seasoning shop and sell us your oily chili peppers at wholesale price. This way, we won't take advantage of your products anymore."

Finally, Tao took their advice and changed her Shihui Restaurant to Guiyang Nanming Tao's Flavor Food Store for selling chili pepper products in November 1994. Her new shop was a great success, but she still provided whatever she had with the oily chili peppers for students when they came. Those students and truck drivers were her most frequent customers. They often bought several bottles at a time for family or later consumption.

That was how the brand Lao Gan Ma started. With the support of government policy, improved transportation, and people's acknowledgment of her reputation, Tao's business developed fast. She refused a lot of invitations to cooperate because she insisted that her brand must only belong to herself.

The popularity of Lao Gan Ma products around the world has a lot to do with the chili pepper. In the middle and late Ming Dynasty (1368–1644), when the Dutch occupied Taiwan, chili peppers came to China and quickly gained popularity, particularly in the South, where they became a necessity in people's daily lives.

Tao sold her oily chili peppers directly from her flavor food store and to restaurants in the Longdongbao area. She wanted to make the business big and successful. She rented two houses in Yunguan Village and hired around forty workers to produce the chili pepper sauce. The procedures were very easy, simply putting the oily chili peppers in glass bottles and sealing them with plastic and strings.

With employees to pay, Tao's need for sales volume increased. She asked the workers to improve their production speed so that more people would become possible consumers of her Lao Gan Ma chili sauce. However, when the stocks in nearby stores and restaurants began to pile up, Tao had to look for new buyers herself. She carried her chili sauce to every food store, small department store, and some company canteens because these target groups could address a large number of consumers simultaneously. To store owners who had not heard about Lao Gan Ma chili sauce, Tao gave them sample products for free. Those owners soon called back to order more after receiving very positive customer responses.

But not all people were so cooperative. Some store owners refused to buy Tao's chili sauce without a proper label. Tao understood she must have corresponding qualifications and go through formal procedures to gain smooth access to the market. At this point, Tao had embarked on the ambitious but thorny path of building her brand and began thinking rationally and long-term.

Stable Progress

An Internal Perspective of Lao Gan Ma Production Workshop

—Chapter Four—

Ensuring Quality from the Source

I n 1996, Tao's business began to grow considerably. She rented a big factory in Yunguan Village. She hired a capable manager named Li, who handled business licenses, organization code certificates, tax registration certificates, food production licenses, sanitation certificates, etc. Many of her old acquaintances joined her production team as well. After that, Tao no longer worried about market demand.

In July 1997, the Asian financial crisis started in Thailand and quickly swept through the global economy. The currencies of Southeast Asian countries depreciated significantly and quickly affected Japan, South Korea, Russia, and some countries in Latin America. Under the impact of this financial crisis, the economic situation of some countries seriously deteriorated, even resulting in political turmoil.

One month later, Guiyang Nanming Lao Gan Ma Flavor Food Co., Ltd. was officially established, and the number of workers expanded to more than 200 people. At that time, Tao did not know whether the financial crisis would affect her business. Still, a series of stable financial policies in China had created a good operating environment for entrepreneurial companies like Tao's.

Starting in 1993, the Chinese government began to implement macro-control in response to the domestic financial chaos, resolutely and effectively suppressing "real estate fever," "development zone fever," and "stock fever" that could have led to bubble economies. In January 1996, the National Financial Work Conference proposed the tasks of "adhering to a moderately tight monetary policy" and "increasing financial supervision, effectively preventing financial risks, and maintaining the legal and stable operation of the financial industry." In January 1997, the National Financial Work Conference proposed that year as the year of preventing financial risks to "effectively rectify the financial order, prevent and resolve financial risks, deepen the reform of the financial system, and significantly improve the operation, management, and service levels of financial enterprises."

The Chinese government's active and responsible attitude won praise from the international community. It promoted the stable growth of China's financial industry and national economy and made a positive contribution to the stable development of finance and economy in Asia and the world.

Tao did not receive much influence from the crisis and devoted herself entirely to her factory. "Focus on your work," she said to her employees, "I will pay you and provide you with meals and residences." Very few private companies at that time provided such benefits for their employees.

No particular celebration was held for the grand opening. Tao only tied a piece of red cloth on the factory gate according to the local custom to wish for a prosperous future.

Tao's factory had about ten huge pots for cooking chili pepper sauce and exhaust fans to ensure ventilation. There were four operation rooms: the material selection room for selecting raw peppers and preliminary processing; the production room, which played a decisive role in producing fried oil peppers; the bottle washing room for cleaning the containers; and the packaging room for preparing the finished products.

The production room was 500–600 square meters. Tao built more than a dozen stoves with refractory bricks and installed large iron pots with a diameter of 1.45 meters on top. These pots could cook up to 50 kilograms of peppers at a time. Formulating and controlling the fire, which Tao's employees lacked, were two essential factors for successfully making the chili sauce. As an inexperienced entrepreneur, Tao led her workers in the cooking process in person and slowly explored efficient ways to manage the factory.

The Irreplaceable "Chili Taster"

T ao placed an extra stove next to the big cooking stoves for herself to develop new products. She was the "chili taster" for Lao Gan Ma chili sauce, like the taster for Kweichow Moutai liquor.

Quality and taste were everything. This was Tao's theory in the food business after selling multiple products. Poor service may affect customers' moods, whereas poor food quality and taste would affect their health and consumption experience and cause a loss of trust in a brand.

Every morning, Tao arrived at her factory early to watch over the production procedures. She examined the fried chili peppers in three steps: color, smell, and taste.

After thousands of improvements, Tao's oily chili has won public recognition. Tao strictly controlled her product quality, refusing to bring unqualified products into the market even if it reduced her profit.

To protect her taste, Tao never drank wine or tea. She could quickly and comprehensively capture and assess the multiple layers of taste in the fried chili peppers. Soon, she and her employees became skillful in their jobs. Workers would put peppers they were cooking in small dishes and hand them to

Tao, who walked around the stoves and gave instructions, such as "This pot needs one more minute" or "This pot is ready." The workers would then immediately carry out her orders. For ready pots, workers would quickly gather to help take out the peppers in time to make sure they were tasty and crunchy. It seemed to be an easy task but was difficult to achieve due to a lack of standards. The fried peppers would then be put aside for cooling for several hours until they became shiny and crunchy.

Tao strictly enforced the requirements of cooking chili peppers at every step. After some time, one of her workers, Liu, came to her and said, "*Laoganma,* you don't need to taste every pot; it's too much for you. We already know how to cook, and our chilies won't be too different from the ones you cook."

Tao replied firmly, "No, I must taste to make sure every pot has the best quality." Later, she asked all her employees to have a stopwatch when they cooked the chili peppers to calculate time more accurately.

Workers Required for a Change

Overconsumption of chili peppers will cause a lot of problems. Traditional Chinese Medicine theory believes that chili peppers will harm the *yin* elements in human bodies like liquor does, resulting in a series of *yang* symptoms. Every day, Tao had to taste the chili sauce dozens or even hundreds of times until her mouth often blistered from inflammation, and she could not distinguish the tastes of any other food. But thanks to her persistence, her chili sauce has never had any quality issues. Many people advised her to use alkali for her sauce like many others did, but Tao insisted on using all-natural ingredients by mixing Zunyi chili peppers and Huaxi chili peppers together to combine spiciness and fragrance at the optimal proportion— Zunyi for heat and Huaxi for aroma. Following the market demand, she also made chicken and beef chili sauces, which received a great response from the buyers.

With work on the production line, issues with licenses, funding, and employment, as well as dealing with various management departments, Tao was extremely busy at that time.

One day, as soon as she entered the factory, some workers in the cleaning section came to her and said, "*Laoganma*, cutting the chili peppers is so hard, and it hurts the eyes so badly. Can you switch us to something else?"

Tao went to the material selection room and showed them how to cut the peppers correctly. "Don't put your face too close to the peppers, and you should be fine. Remember to wash your hands immediately after cutting so that you won't accidentally touch your face or eyes with the pepper smell on them," she said, "Every job here is not easy. Look at me; my mouth blisters because I've been tasting the pepper every day. Do you hear me complain? How about those who fry the peppers in front of a big fire every day? Do they not find it difficult?"

Hearing this, the workers said, "You're right, *laoganma*. We'll try your method." They soon got the hang of it and solved the problem. Similarly, Tao always personally taught anyone who encountered difficulties at work to help them overcome them. They were like a big family. On the first Mid-Autumn Festival after the factory was established, Tao told the workers, "Everyone, go to the finance department after work today and get 200 *yuan*. Have a happy holiday!" From then on, she would prepare gifts and awards for her employees at every festival.

Trouble with the Packaging Manufacturer

As soon as she received the license for the factory, Tao began preparing to package her chili sauce for marketing. The packaging industry in Guizhou was not as developed as today, and the only place to buy the glass bottles needed to contain the sauce was the Guiyang No. 2 Glass Factory.

In the past, Tao simply put the chili sauce directly in her customers' containers or in plastic bags for some starch jelly stores. However, standardized containers had to be provided if she wanted to sell her chili sauce nationwide. Her bottles needed to have proper size openings, big enough for utensils and small enough for proper sealing.

Tao had been coming to this glass factory to purchase glass bottles since 1995. Mao Liwei, the factory owner, remembered that she only bought several dozen at a time, which was too trivial a number to benefit the factory, with an annual production of glass bottles over 18,000 tons.

Tao's first visit to the factory was quite challenging. Not believing the woman carrying two baskets was a factory owner, the security guard refused to let her in. Tao did not get angry at him but waited patiently until the owner allowed her in. But after the owner expressed reluctance about her order, she hurriedly inquired, "No baby is born adult-size; you need to give them time to grow! I can't go back if I don't get the bottles today." Mao thought for a moment and agreed. He never dreamed that this inconspicuous woman would completely change the future of his factory. By 2003, the No. 2 Glass Factory's two production lines could not meet the demand from Lao Gan Ma alone. It has now expanded to over 10,000 square meters with four production lines that function 24 hours a day to produce 35,000 tons of glass bottles annually.

Paying on the Spot

After selling out her first batch of goods, Tao realized that she had to sell the leftover products in stock quickly to avoid a backlog of funds. She and her workers thus advertised Lao Gan Ma chili sauce in restaurants, supermarkets, and school dining facilities. Tao told her employees to be clear about their costs and profits when talking to the buyers. Many store owners were pleased with Lao Gan Ma chili sauce and were happy to promote it to others, but some first buyers were cautious. "I know your chili sauce is good," they said to Tao, "but we haven't bought it before, so we don't know how much we can profit from it."

Tao would answer, "Just put some on your shelves, and don't worry about paying me if you can't make money from it. I'll come take the rest back." In this way, Lao Gan Ma opened its local market one store at a time.

Just when Mr. Mao, owner of No. 2 Glass Factory, was about to forget about Tao, she surprised him by coming back and making two big orders of several thousand bottles. This changed Mao's opinion toward Tao, and he began to treat her as a serious customer.

With the problem of packaging solved, Tao focused on her raw materials. Cutting off the chili roots was a small but time-consuming procedure in the whole chili sauce production process. Tao hoped she could find suppliers who could cut off the roots for her, so she went to Xiazi County, the biggest producer of high-quality chili peppers in China. The workers in Xiazi County used to string large numbers of chili peppers in bundles for sale, but they stopped doing that when the market demand increased.

Tao bought huge quantities of chili peppers at Xiazi County in Zunyi, Guizhou, under two conditions. First, suppliers must provide her with processed peppers without roots. Second, all peppers must be of high quality. She offered regular market prices for the suppliers and assured them of payment issues. "I always pay full price on the spot as long as the materials are good," she said. In addition to chili peppers, Tao also had strict requirements for oil. Many sellers sold palm oil or others as rapeseed oil, so Tao always checked the sources of her oil carefully for the best taste of her chili sauce.

At this point, many supermarkets and restaurants in other provinces began to reach out to Tao and order Lao Gan Ma chili sauce, so Tao immediately called No. 2 Glass Factory and ordered tens of thousands of bottles.

Always Be with the Workers

As Lao Gan Ma's company size expanded from 200 people to 1,200, Tao's eldest son, Guishan, quit his job and helped his mother with the company. Tao told him that he could make rules but should always consider employees' feelings and treat them as family. She dined with her workers and encouraged the young ones to eat more. Some of her employees said, "*Laoganma* is not like some self-presumptuous parvenus who look down upon others. She treats us as family." When someone criticized that it was inappropriate for a factory owner to dine with her employees or even serve them when they eat, Tao said angrily, "They are my family. They were with me when I started the business, and they were the ones who helped me make Lao Gan Ma the way it is today." Because of her trust and care, her employees were all very dedicated to their work.

Tao followed two principles in her career. One was to be grateful to the ones who helped her, and the other was to be honest with her products. She strictly controlled every step throughout the production process, personally supervising everything from the frying temperature and the humidity of packaging to the size of the bottles.

The year 1997 was a turning point for Lao Gan Ma, not only because of the changing of the name from "Guiyang Nanming Tao's Flavor Food Factory" to "Guiyang Nanming Lao Gan Ma Flavor Food Co., Ltd.," but also because of the changing of a small workshop to a formalized food company. It was not a pure coincidence that Tao chose to establish her company in 1997. With the government's support in vigorously developing non-public ownership in 1996, Lao Gan Ma and many other private enterprises flourished. Despite being illiterate, Tao's diligence and dedication helped her know the economic environment and government policies. Every morning, Tao arrived at her factory before 7:00 a.m. to inform all employees about the day's work and had breakfast with them. At 6:00 p.m., she finished work with everyone, had dinner, and asked the managers about that day's production situation. After that, she would turn on the television to watch *Xinwen Lianbo*, the daily news program produced by China Central TV, and learn about the country's latest policies and the latest trends in economic development.

Resolution for the Idle Workers

As Lao Gan Ma's purchase of chili peppers increased, it created a new job among the Xiazi County suppliers called "the cutters" due to the requirement to provide rootless chili peppers. The job was easy, but the workload was extremely heavy and could not be replaced by machines, so a group of 4,000–5,000 professional cutters was formed, consisting of children, old people, and women who could not find jobs.

The suppliers were very proud of their cutters because they could prepare tens of thousands *jin*[*] of chili peppers overnight. The entire household would participate in the job and have all the peppers cleanly cut and packed the next morning. In addition,

---

[*] One *jin* equals 500 g, or 1.1 pounds.

more truck drivers and stevedores were hired to load and deliver the peppers all year round.

Over the years, Tao had always ordered bottles from her first supplier for old-time's sake. The Guiyang No. 2 Glass Factory was restructured in 1998 and survived the wave of bankruptcy of state-owned enterprises. Its owner never expected that Tao, the woman who pleaded for dozens of bottles, would one day become its most important customer. Today, Lao Gan Ma uses more than one million glass bottles every day, and 60% of that comes from Guiyang No. 2 Glass Factory, while the others are supplied by large enterprises in Chongqing, Zhengzhou, and other places.

With the increasing scale of Lao Gan Ma's production, Tao's career is no longer her own or her family's but tens of thousands of people's.

Market Layout

Products and Marketing

-Chapter Five-

From a Minor Part to a Star

T he most famous spicy food in China is from Guizhou, Sichuan, and Hunan. People's love for chili peppers in these provinces makes it a daily necessity in their lives. It is thus not surprising that Lao Gan Ma's chili sauces became increasingly welcomed in those regions.

Tao's early customers were the ones who first learned about Lao Gan Ma's reputation, as well as truck drivers traveling near Longdongbao. These were the first promoters of Lao Gan Ma, and some even became its dealers. There was a time when Lao Gan Ma's supply of products exceeded demand, and many people waited in long lines until late at night. Tao provided them with hot water, steamed buns, and her chili sauce.

Despite the growth, the imbalance between supply and demand occurred from time to time. Tao decided to build a marketing team for the backlog of goods. Among them, Manager Li was creative, eloquent, bold, and had clear thinking and working experience in state-owned enterprises. He often went to other places to sell Lao Gan Ma products by himself, and with his team, he quickly found a way out for the products. When seeing store owners eating in restaurants, the marketing team would immediately offer some Lao Gan Ma chili sauce, and they promised to charge only when the customers were satisfied after they had tried the products. Slowly, more and more store owners began to accept Lao Gan Ma chili sauce and even sold it to other stores for profit, and some changed their businesses to Lao Gan Ma chili sauce shops.

Tao believed in marketing, but she believed more in quality. So, she required her marketing team to be clear about the product's features when advocating. Chili peppers are good for keeping the body warm, promoting digestion, anti-inflammation, and analgesia. After the reform and opening-up period, people's mobility across the country increased, and people's preferences for food also changed. As the number of people who ate spicy food continued to increase, Tao's consumers also expanded by over 500 million people, from the traditional chili consumption areas (Hunan, Jiangxi, Sichuan, Guizhou, Guangxi, etc.) to the whole country.

At the same time, the fast-food industry developed rapidly worldwide due to the accelerating work pace, and the demand for dehydrated vegetables, including chili peppers, grew. The appearance of low-fat and spicy food and the demand for healthy food changed people's eating habits. Three-quarters of the world population now eat chili peppers or chili products, making chili peppers one of the most consumed vegetables worldwide.

Tao didn't know about the advantages and great potential of her business at first. Still, as she gradually realized how big the chili pepper market was, she insisted on ensuring her product's high quality and low price. She knew by heart that sacrificing quality would mean disaster for a company. Some years ago, there was a very successful liquor company in Tao's hometown, and it became a trend to give this type of liquor to friends and families as gifts. However, in only a year or two, everyone stopped buying this liquor, which used to be sold in every mall, store, and restaurant, because the company's fraudulent behavior of adding water to increase volume was exposed.

Therefore, Tao forbade her company from selling unqualified products. She never believed in pure marketing without quality that's worth the customers' money. In the food industry, quality matters for consumers' health and determines an enterprise's fate.

Is Advertising Essential?

Tao emphasized product quality but also acknowledged the importance of expanding sales. After many years of experimenting, she realized that in business, it was necessary to allow others to profit while the company's profits were ensured.

Tao had many business partners because of her and her employees' honest work styles, but Lao Gan Ma developed further demand for external sales. Therefore, since 1998, the company has been sending employees to attend training on advanced business management in Guangzhou, Shanghai, Shenzhen, and other coastal cities. After that, it began to formulate its own business indicators and performance appraisal plans.

Many people at that time knew the story of Tao and her chili sauce, and some even dreamed of meeting Tao in person. One day, some people came to visit her when she was tasting the samples in the factory. It was an old customer with some merchants from Hunan who were excited to meet the "legendary *laoganma*." Tao brought them some of her chili sauce while explaining that she was no legend at all.

"Geez!" exclaimed one of the merchants after tasting it, slapping it on the table and startling Tao, "*Laoganma*, your chili sauce is amazing! I've never had better chili sauce in my life!"

Another merchant followed, "*Laoganma*, can you give a few dozen of your samples? I'll sell them in Hunan, and I can be your dealer if the market there is good!"

"Sure, take a hundred, and we can talk business if they're good," said Tao. The merchants insisted on paying for the samples, so Tao gave them some extra as gifts.

Several months later, the merchants came back and brought Tao some good news. The samples that they brought back to Hunan sold out in all test sales points by the next day. After some further market research, the merchants returned to Guiyang and offered to be the general agents of Lao Gan Ma in Hunan.

Tao was pleasantly surprised. She brought the merchants to her factory, showed them her production procedures, and explained her rules for producing and selling. Happy and satisfied with the quality of Lao Gan Ma chili sauce, the merchants assured Tao, "*Laoganma*, just leave Hunan to us, and we'll open its market for you."

"No," said Tao, "you're not opening that market for me but for you. My rule is to always pay on the spot. It's not that I don't trust you. I do it with all my partners and suppliers. I don't owe anyone money, so I don't accept credit from others either."

Hearing this, the merchants looked hesitant. Tao continued, "If you want to be my agents, you must believe in Lao Gan Ma's products. I promise you that my product will bring you profit." Finally, the merchants paid for the first batch of goods, and Tao agreed to have them be her only agents in Hunan. "I give the Hunan market to you, so you should protect Lao Gan Ma's brand like your own name. I will not forget your contributions to the company."

When Questionable Products Went to Market

At the beginning of her business, Tao successfully increased sales without advertising. She established her distribution channels, remained open and up to date with useful experiences, and emphasized cultivating new talents in the company.

During that time, most Chinese people were still not used to the growing importance of business in society and tended to despise profit-driven values.

A story that circulated widely at that time described a popular toothpaste company with decent quality and exquisite design that inevitably fell into a sales crisis after several years of development. A young man said to the desperate chairman, "I have an important advice for you on this piece of paper worthy of 50,000 *yuan*." The chairman finally bought the man's advice on the piece of paper, which read, "Increase the opening of the tube by one millimeter." This advice successfully solved the company's problem with an unprecedented sale that year.

The general attitude toward that story was negative, thinking that what the toothpaste company did was deceptive to its customers. While the individual buyers might have bought more toothpaste out of their trust in the company, they would eventually stop buying after realizing the lack of actual benefits in the change.

While most people considered a "business value" despicable, Tao disagreed because her values were based on good products, low prices, and small profits. These values played an important role in Lao Gan Ma's success, making the brand invincible over the years. As a smart and experienced businesswoman, Tao learned to balance between small and long-term profits well. In 2001, one glass factory provided Lao Gan Ma with 800 sets of containers, each consisting of 32 glass bottles. However, customers soon reported that these containers were not sealed properly. Tao took it seriously and asked to recover the entire batch quickly. Some managers suggested resealing the bottles rather than destroying them due to the large number of goods, but Tao firmly opposed this idea in order to protect the company's reputation in the long run.

Keeping Profits Small

Back in her days selling vegetables, Tao always gave her customers something small for free after they paid. Slowly, more and more people came to her vendor for vegetables, and she always finished earlier than the other sellers. When she was a restaurant owner, Tao also followed the principle of benefiting every customer, which laid the foundation for her success. After she started selling the chili sauce and achieved some notable results, some of her dealers asked if the company could now raise the price for further profits, to which Tao firmly answered, "No!"

"But why?" they asked. Tao explained that a businessman could earn one cent from a thousand people, but he must never earn ten dollars from one. "Then, let's spend some money on advertising on TV and newspaper," they again suggested. Tao answered that Lao Gan Ma did not need any advertisement aside from its products. She could not allow her customers to pay higher prices for her chili sauce with better advertisements and in fancier packages, which were all unnecessary if the sauce was good.

As Lao Gan Ma's marketing team explored the domestic market, they always strived to have the target customers try their product as soon as possible, and many of them became the company's regional agents directly afterward. Soon, Lao Gan Ma had its general agents in Beijing, Wuhan, and Guangzhou. In two to three years, Lao Gan Ma products covered all markets in China except for Taiwan and even exported to the US, Australia, South Africa, and Southeast Asia.

Many people said, "*Laoganma*, you are amazing. You have created a national logo all by yourself!"

Tao said, "What do I know about the logo? All I'm doing is making chili sauce."

"It's ok, *laoganma*. You don't need a logo. You *are* the logo!"

Tao and her company focused on making chili pepper-related products that she was good at, and her professionalism and persistence made Lao Gan Ma the only brand of chili sauces and oils for many people. It was clean, delicious, and affordable.

While many people advised Tao to change Lao Gan Ma's package so that the customers did not get aesthetically tired of its look, Tao believed that the package should not be the focus of an enterprise. "If I were a customer," she said, "I wanted to know how the product was, how the price was, not how beautiful the package was."

Some people wondered why Lao Gan Ma often stopped production, which was not often seen in other big enterprises. Tao explained that the company would cease production whenever a safety issue appeared to avoid unqualified products from entering the market. Her willingness to sacrifice her own profit for customers' consumption experience assured her reputation and customer sources. Additionally, she would also cease production if the raw material had any problem despite the market demand.

Once, due to urgent sales needs, Lao Gan Ma ordered ten tons of fermented soybeans from Chongqing, and the quality inspector did not have time to thoroughly examine the goods before sending them to the workshops. But Tao insisted on checking the soybeans carefully. When she stirred the beans, she noticed that many had gone bad. Immediately, she informed all workshops to stop using soybeans and contacted the factory in Chongqing. It turned out that the supplier hid a lot of spoiled beans under the good ones for convenience. They explained that the beans were processed in a particular way and were thus still edible, but Tao knew that only the good beans could render the desired taste and ensure the safety of consumers.

"I will not take such a risk to harm the reputation of Lao Gan Ma. I have never given you counterfeit money; why do you give me a spoiled product?" she asked the supplier, who tried to persuade her to accept the goods at a lower price. Tao refused. She returned the goods and initiated the process to terminate her contract with the supplier. Meanwhile, she ordered the company to stop production until new soybeans were supplied.

Later, when her dealers called to ask about the delay, Tao explained the danger of sacrificing quality for sales. "The two-day wait is worthwhile for our company in the long run." The dealers then explained this to the customers, who also found it convincing.

Lao Gan Ma's First Dealer

Jiang Yuanzhi was the general manager of Shanghai Mebo Foods Co., Ltd. and one of the first Lao Gan Ma dealers. When asked about the brand, she said, "I think the taste of Lao

Gan Ma is pretty much the same as it was in the beginning. It's truly a conscientious enterprise and will not change its focus on product quality because of cast or raw materials."

Jiang started cooperating with Lao Gan Ma in 1998, and she witnessed the whole developmental process of the brand.

Tao insisted on transacting money and delivering goods on the spot with her dealers. At first, some dealers were worried that they might not always have enough money ready for purchase, so Tao allowed them to pay a deposit first.

Some dealers once suggested Tao adjust the taste of Lao Gan Ma chili sauce for consumers in certain areas, to which Tao refused. "If I change it, it will not be Lao Gan Ma chili sauce anymore, and people will not like it anymore." Over the years, the type of chili sauce with the most balanced flavor of fragrance, spiciness, and grain taste that Tao had initially designed proved to be most welcomed, while the others with different formulas were all gradually eliminated.

Based on Tao's sales philosophy of small profits and quick returns, Lao Gan Ma chili sauce's prices range from 5 to 20 *yuan*. The dealers all agreed on this price range, which both allowed profits and ensured customers.

To her dealers, Tao entrusted the regional markets and promised never to restrict their development as long as they achieved positive growth. This way, her dealers sincerely valued their market shares and were very devoted to the company.

Lao Gan Ma dealers were extremely meticulous in their marketing work and severely cracked down on counterfeit products. During special events, the sales terminals would prepare for type genus and direct mail advertising in time.

Tao once told her employees and partners, "People say all merchants are treachery. I don't believe in that. I never lie to my customers. Please remember, our company must always win with integrity in market competition." The secret to Lao Gan Ma's success was simple. She never forgot her childhood lesson that she must always be diligent and honest and never brag or lie.

Selling Chili Sauce to Cantonese People

With the support of the marketing team, Lao Gan Ma could focus more on product innovation and brand building. With its advanced economy, Guangzhou (Canton) was a key area for the company's planning and development. However, Guangzhou cuisine was very mild compared to Guizhou's taste, so exploring the Guangzhou market was also bound to be a tough breakthrough.

Tao was well aware of the challenge. While Lao Gan Ma's overall sales volume was around 200 million *yuan*, she did not expect the sales share of Guangzhou to be more than 10 million. The dealer in Guangzhou, on the other hand, set the goal at 30 million, and he promised, "If Lao Gan Ma can sell in other provinces, it will sell too in Guangzhou."

Tao felt such a goal was too unrealistic, but she also knew that dealer well and knew him as a frank, hard-working person. So, she said to him in front of everyone, "If you achieve this goal next year, I will award you a car."

"*Laoganma*, you didn't even buy yourself a car. Will you really be so generous to buy one for someone else?" someone joked.

"You'll see," answered Tao.

Everyone took it as a joke, but not Tao. She understood how a 30-million-*yuan* sales-share in Guangzhou would expand the overall market for the brand. If Lao Gan Ma's customer group could cover Guangzhou, it could also reach out to Hong Kong, Macau, and international regions. Looking back, focusing on the Guangzhou market was of great significance to the development of the Lao Gan Ma Company. On the one hand, this expanded the local consumer market and guided local consumption habits. On the other hand, it played the role of product exhibition and sales, greatly promoting the spread of Lao Gan Ma products across the country. Guangzhou has also become the most important strategic base for Lao Gan Ma in the national and even international market layout.

Tao remembered the commitment between her and the Guangzhou dealer. By the end of the second year, she asked the marketing department about the annual sales in Guangzhou that year and was told that the promised 30-million-*yuan* goal was met. Tao immediately called the Guangzhou dealer to congratulate him and bought him a Volkswagen Jetta sedan on behalf of the company.

The dealer was surprised because he did not believe that Tao was serious about that. Everyone else was shocked and said, "*Laoganma*, you shouldn't spend so much money on awards. You haven't even bought yourself a car. We know you're living a frugal life, and no one will blame you if you don't buy us anything."

Tao replied, "It's not about being generous or not. It's about keeping one's promise." When the dealer received the car key from Tao, his hands were shaking with excitement and gratitude. After that, all dealers were impressed by Tao's integrity and trusted her more. Lao Gan Ma's sales in Guangzhou also improved and changed the tastes of many people there.

How to Be Attractive?

While the southern market was developing smoothly, the northern market encountered some unexpected difficulties. Lao Gan Ma had larger distributors in the North, and the major supermarkets and stores, such as Walmart and Carrefour, were all selling Lao Gan Ma products, but the sales volume remained low. After a market survey, some local dealers reflected that people did not like to buy Lao Gan Ma because it did not have promoters and its packaging was too provincial and unattractive.

Tao did not understand why the appearance of a food product should be the cause for its appeal. It turned out that certain brands would have special staff members in supermarkets to promote their products. The inspection team from Henan reported that these promoters would persuade customers to buy their products instead of Lao Gan Ma by comparing their packages, "Lao Gan Ma is a popular brand, but you can see that it's not appealing both on the inside and the outside. Our products are obviously tastier just by their looks, and we have better packaging if you want to use them as gifts."

Tao discussed this problem with the managers of different departments, and many people believed that Lao Gan Ma's packaging should be improved. Tao, on the other hand, was against the idea, arguing that changing the packaging would lead to a price increase and ultimately unhealthy competition against the other companies on packaging instead of the chili sauce itself. Tao also denied the suggestion of hiring promoters because it was against her marketing principle. "Lao Gan Ma's advantages are good taste and low price. Having promoters means a higher cost. We must never let customers pay unnecessary money."

"*Laoganma*, we can't expect to have everything we want at the same time, right? We need to accept changes if they are necessary," someone said.

Tao fell into thought. What was the thing that she really wanted? She recalled her days in Shihui Restaurant. People liked coming there for the food and the free chili sauce. Tasty and affordable. Changing those would change the foundation of Lao Gan Ma's brand. Finally, she decided to fully take advantage of its "disadvantage" to make its "unappealing-ness" and "provinciality" its biggest feature.

She told her dealers to put up a slogan wherever Lao Gan Ma chili sauce was sold, "My Packaging Only Costs 3 Cents." This statement responded powerfully to disparaging comments from promoters of other companies and successfully opened the northern market. Consumers quickly spread the news about this tasty and multifunctional chili sauce, and the sales volume of Lao Gan Ma increased significantly, giving its competitors an insurmountable disadvantage.

Some people asked Tao, "Why do you insist on having your dealers pay first before sending them the products? Other companies are all eager to give their goods to dealers as soon as possible."

"People also ask me why Lao Gan Ma doesn't have advertisement or marketing activities, or why our shipping units are so big, and why we refuse small orders," replied Tao. "It's because our products are good, and our customers like them. We keep our profits to the minimum so that the customers can have the optimal consuming experience. That's why we don't use any of the promotional methods."

Actively Protecting Rights

Copycats

—Chapter Six—

Three Characters Are Enough

What is your greatest happiness in this life? Tao's answer to this question was, "My success in my career."

Tao was illiterate, and she used to draw a circle to represent her signature on documents. Later, her colleagues suggested she learn to write her own name for safety. They wrote her name, "Tao Hua Bi," on paper and told her to practice writing it in her free time. "These three characters are so difficult!" she exclaimed. She practiced writing them like a little child for three days. "It's harder than cutting chili peppers." Three days later, when she could finally write her own name, she treated the entire staff to a meal. These three characters are the only ones she knows up until today.

Tao worked hard every day because she wanted her life to be meaningful. One day, her sons took her on a trip, but she felt extremely uncomfortable when she left the company. She said she could not sleep while away from the cooking sounds in the workshops. She did not know enjoyment, only responsibilities. She cared about the several thousands of people in her company, and she never felt prouder when her company was awarded as an exemplary taxpayer.

In 1998, Lao Gan Ma had already established its own king-dom. As the company expanded, Tao knew that she must change her management style.

While she had not received much education, Tao knew the importance of knowledge. Therefore, she sent her sons and employees to learn from other companies' advanced experiences in Guangzhou, Shanghai, Shenzhen, and other places.

Tao also asked her employees not to accept interviews or to publicize how well they were doing because Lao Gan Ma was not a movie star, and it did not need public attention to make high-quality chili sauce. Excessive attention could also cause jealousy, conspiracy, and cheating.

However, as the company's reputation grew, Tao's story became widely known, and the contrast between her illiteracy and her company's huge success became the focus of media reports. Some described Tao in the following words, "She is not as well-informed as urban professionals but has business acumen and a unique vision that surpasses urban elites; she is a woman, but she is as decisive and perseverant as a man; she does not know any modern management wisdom, but she manages her business in an orderly manner and has high morale; she does not engage in fancy advertising and marketing, but she sells her products well all over the country and all over the world, making an ordinary food condiment into a well-known brand at home and abroad ... "

Soon afterward, Tao received notice that some companies were also producing Lao Gan Ma illegally. The need to apply for a trademark and logo was urgent. However, the process was far from smooth. Lao Gan Ma's application was rejected three times in 1996 and 1998 by the Trademark Office of China National Intellectual Property Administration (hereinafter referred to as Trademark Office) due to "lacking prominent features, because *laoganma* is a common name in daily life."

But why could similar brands like *kangshifu* (Master Kang), *hongdama* (Aunt Hong), and *axiangpo* (Granny Axiang) be approved? Tao did not accept this explanation, and she continued to apply every time her application was rejected. On January 25, 1999, after it was rejected the third time, Lao Gan Ma submitted a review application to the Trademark Office. As she struggled to settle the problem with the trademark, counterfeit Lao Gan Ma products popped up all over the country.

The Danger of Unprotected Profit

Tao could not legally protect her brand without a trademark. Since 1997, there have been more than sixty copycat companies in various provinces, including Hunan, Sichuan, Shaanxi, Gansu, and Guizhou, selling similar chili sauces to Lao Gan Ma's. With their almost identical packaging, they easily confused many customers, who began to think that the quality of Lao Gan Ma chili sauce had deteriorated. Lao Gan Ma suffered considerable financial and reputation losses, but Tao had no other way but to seek support from the Industrial and Commercial Departments.

Despite all adversities, Tao believed that these were the necessary conditions for a company's success. As a self-made businesswoman, Tao greatly cherished her work and was not intimidated by knockoffs, whom she had been dealing with since the time she ran the Shihui Restaurant. "You better watch out if you don't stop selling my stuff right now," she would warn the copycats whenever she heard of one. In 1994, when she started her business, she put the name Lao Gan Ma on her packaging to promote her products. A name was a brand, a mark, and what kept a company alive. Tao devoted her whole life to this brand and would not allow anyone to steal it easily or for free.

But her right could not be guaranteed before she could register the trademark for Lao Gan Ma, and people never stopped trying to exploit the tempting benefits close at hand. Some small manufacturers blatantly counterfeited the chili sauce, but Lao Gan Ma Company always managed to report them as soon as it found out. Later, some manufacturers decided to legalize the brand Lao Gan Ma, which created a more serious problem.

Someone Took Lao Gan Ma's Trademark

In September 1997, a new Lao Gan Ma company was registered in Hunan.

Two months after its establishment, the company signed a production contract with Guiyang Nanming Tangmeng Food Factory to provide production technology. Hunan Huayue Food Co., Ltd. (hereinafter referred to as Hunan Huayue Company), on the other hand, provided equipment, facilities, and space to jointly produce Lao Gan Ma flavored chili sauce, which was sold on the market that month.

Now that there were two Lao Gan Ma companies, both manufacturing in Guiyang, people could not easily tell which was the authentic brand anymore.

One day, when Tao was busy working in the workshops as usual, her marketing manager ran in and shouted, "*Laoganma*, something very bad happened!"

"What is it? Calm down first!"

"There's another Lao Gan Ma in Hunan!"

"What's so special about that? We've seen lots of fake Lao Gan Mas already. Just report them to the related department."

"Not this time. They are taking your brand away!"

This time, Tao panicked.

Tao had been using a special sticker to label her chili sauce since she opened the Shihui Restaurant. The sticker was red with a white oval pattern centering her picture; under it was the name *laoganma* written by a calligraphy enthusiast from Guiyang, the company's name, and brief slogans highlighting the product in the form of couplets, "Shihui Restaurant," "flavored soybeans," "fragrant and spicy," "elegant and exquisite," "Guizhou specialty," "high quality." Each character was contained in yellow oval circles. In addition, the product description could be found on the left, and information regarding the formula, execution standards, company address, and phone number could be found on the right.

Tao liked red because it represented the chili pepper, the national flag, and a happy, prosperous life.

She quickly called for a meeting to discuss solutions regarding this new crisis brought by the copycat Lao Gan Ma company in Hunan. For days, she could not sleep at night, wondering how the business that she started from scratch could not be hers and why she could not prevent it from being stolen. Without an approved trademark, Lao Gan Ma was like the meat on someone's chopping block. If the Hunan Lao Gan Ma won the battle, there would soon be more Lao Gan Mas in Chengdu, Guangzhou, Beijing, Nanjing, and other places ... and the brand would thus be destroyed due to unsupervised quality.

Tao believed in the government's ability to regulate the market and prohibit such acts of appropriating the fruits of other people's labor. Nevertheless, she did not know if the government could still protect her rights if the copycat company did not violate the law.

After some time, Tao changed her company's name and tried to apply for a design patent for the packaging with the new name on it. Intellectual property experts suggested going to the copyright office to register copyright first rather than applying for a patent, which required more time. Once Lao Gan Ma had its copyright, it could choose to seek legal support. After changing its name in November 1997, Lao Gan Ma Company applied for a design patent to the National Patent Office for its packaging and got approved on August 22, 1998. In addition, Lao Gan Ma Company also registered copyright with the Guizhou Provincial Copyright Bureau on December 30, 1997.

At the same time, the copycat Lao Gan Ma in Hunan took advantage of advertisements to improve visibility. In April 1998, the Hunan Huayue Company terminated its contract with Guiyang Nanming Tangmeng Food Factory and carried out production independently. Their products were awarded honorary certificates with the highest market share in Hunan. The company announced that they had spent a total of 2.7 million *yuan* in advertising to promote their Lao Gan Ma flavored soybean chili sauce. When Tao's company was applying for a trademark, Hunan Huayue Company was also applying for one for the same product.

Tao's company started its application in December 1997 and received the design patent on August 22, 1998. In contrast, the Hunan company started late on January 20, 1998, and received the patent for the design that they started using since their cooperation with Guiyang Nanming Tangmeng Factory only on October 10, 1998.

Tao's confidence started to grow. She was determined to win this war, and she must win.

The year 1998 was rough for Tao as it was for a lot of people, with floods occurring throughout the Yangtze River basin and the continuous storms at the Dongting and Poyang Lakes that rapidly increased the river flow. Tao was exhausted by the excessive work in the factory and the business battlefield. She yearned for a normal person's life, for the safety of family members and herself. The appearance of Hunan Lao Gan Ma was a heavy blow to Tao because it broke her values of diligence and integrity. As her health deteriorated, Tao had to pause her company's production and go to the hospital, leaving the phone ringing from her dealers all over the country asking for goods.

Protecting Her Brand

The girl who once worked in the Shihui Restaurant, "Peter Pan," was now a general distributor of Lao Gan Ma. She hurriedly came to visit Tao when she heard about her illness.

"How much money do you make in a year?" Tao asked her.

"About a million."

"Good, I'm proud of you. You are not a little girl in school anymore. You can take care of yourself."

Tao sighed. "Peter Pan" had never seen her so sad and hopeless about life. In her memory, *laoganma* Tao never complained about anything; all she did was work. Now, her mental strength burned out, and she collapsed. She talked to "Peter Pan" like an old friend for a long time and said, "I don't want to fight anymore. I've made enough money for my family. What's the meaning of all these struggles?"

"No problem, *ganma*. Let's just live. You deserve to live a happy life," said "Peter Pan."

"But what about resuming production?" asked the marketing team, "The dealers are all asking about the goods."

"No need. It's pointless," answered Tao.

"Why?"

"I'm too old and tired to fight anymore. I am satisfied with what I have …" Angry, disappointed, and heartbroken, Tao added, "I want to live like a normal person."

Her staff around her nodded. They understood that she had had too much pressure since the beginning of the crisis with the company brand.

"Don't worry about it, *ganma*. You don't need to do it if you don't want to. Think about the time when Brothers Guishan and

Hui get married and have children; how great will that be!" said "Peter Pan," and Tao finally smiled. "Peter Pan" watched that smile and realized that her *laoganma* hadn't smiled for a long time.

Just then, "Peter Pan's" phone rang. "What? Fake products in Hubei?!" Tao heard her shout over the phone and felt anxious again. "Wait, you said real products? From Hunan Lao Gan Ma? I see." "Peter Pan" hung up and returned with the news that the Lao Gan Ma company in Hunan had taken advantage of their recent suspension of production and supplied some of their goods to the Lao Gan Ma dealers.

Tao was shocked and outraged, and her determination to protect her company's reputation returned. She jumped out of bed, pulled out the infusion needle, and went back to the company with her staff. With "Peter Pan," Tao told her to return to Hubei and stop the dealers from selling the fake products from the copycat company at all costs. Tao, on the other hand, would do her best to produce the needed goods in time.

On their way back to the company, Tao asked Manager Li why the company in Hunan could still violate their rights even after they had acquired the design patent. "I'm not sure," answered Li, "I can go to Hubei in person and investigate." Tao agreed and told him to collect any evidence of infringement for later use. Later, Tao told her staff to cheer up and go back to work. "Lao Gan Ma is invincible. We will always get up even if we are beaten to the ground."

When she was alone in her office, Tao carefully compared her company's design and that of the copycat. The only difference between the two designs was the frame's shape around Tao's picture—Guiyang's was oval, and Hunan's was diamond. Just then, a manager came in with some bad news, "The Hunan Lao Gan Ma's trademark registration was approved."

"What trademark?"

"The trademark for 'Liu Xiangqiu Lao Gan Ma.' They registered the 30th category of goods, completely covering the condiment industry."

"When was it approved?"

"December 1."

"How about our application?"

"It was approved, too, on December 31."

In frustration, Tao threw some fruit she was holding on the table. She had to see her original brand registered as someone else's.

Her staff also found some reports online about the two Lao Gan Ma companies. The introduction about Guiyang Lao Gan Ma read,

The title *laoganma* of Guiyang Lao Gan Ma Company comes from Tao Huabi's philanthropic attitude. Tao Huabi, a native of Yongxing Township, Meitan County, Guizhou Province, dropped out of school at an early age because of poverty, and she often cooked at home. With a family tradition of cooking and an eagerness to learn, she mastered the skill of making condiments. Later, she settled in Guiyang with her husband, who worked in the Geological Team. In the early 1980s, after her husband unfortunately passed away, Tao tried to make ends meet for her two young children by opening a starch jelly stall and then a restaurant. She served a unique soybean chili sauce, which made her business boom. During this time, a student at Guiyang Technical School often came to eat. Tao took care of him and his fellow schoolmates out of compassion, not only allowing them to eat for free but also helping them complete their studies. The students were deeply touched and called Tao their *ganma*. Others also began to call Tao *laoganma* out of respect. The name *laoganma* thus spread, and Tao's real name was even forgotten. *Laoganma* became the synonym for Tao's chili sauce, which was extremely well received, and when Tao was mass-producing this product, she named it "Lao Gan Ma." This has become a fact to the locals after being reported by the media several times in recent years.

The introduction about Hunan Lao Gan Ma read,

During the Warlord Era in the early Republic of China, General Tang Shengzhi, a native of Dong'an, Hunan, was a connoisseur of Hunan cuisine. He promoted the traditional Hunan dish Dong'an Chicken and formed the branch of Hunan cuisine, Tangjia Cuisine. The real success of Tangjia Cuisine was a series of condiments made by *laoganma*, whose husband was a famous chef in the Tang household. According to the Hunan Huayue Company, Liu Xiangqiu is from Hunan and has mastered the craftsmanship of *laoganma*. The company's Lao Gan Ma products are related to her craftsmanship.

The so-called "Lao Gan Ma products" by Hunan Huayue Company were clearly stated at the beginning to have used the technology of Guiyang Nanming Tangmeng Food Factory, as evidenced by the contract. How come they were now relating them to the craftsmanship of a Hunan *laoganma*? Tao was furious.

After some time, the Lao Gan Ma company in Hunan reached out to cooperate with Tao's company. Tao firmly rejected this, saying there was no room for negotiation. Lao Gan Ma was established by Tao alone, and no one could infringe on it. "They stole from me, and now they are thinking of discussing how to divide my stuff with me? No way!" She would rather keep fighting until she lost the company than give it to someone else for free.

Guizhou media was also in an uproar after the two Lao Gan Ma trademarks were approved. If there could be two Lao Gan Mas in the market, could there also be three? Or four? If so, how should the market be regulated? If not, then what was the standard for approving and denying trademark registration?

Tao was not afraid, and she knew she must not conciliate. Seeking legal support was her only solution, and she believed in the justice of the law. Since the reform and opening-up, China has gradually established a socialist market economic system, and the degree of marketization has been greatly improved. Although some people would take advantage of legal loopholes, marketization and theorization were important cornerstones for community development that ensured a healthy market economy.

Tao consulted a lawyer, who said that in accordance with relevant laws and regulations, Lao Gan Ma Company could submit a trademark review application to the Trademark Office and file a lawsuit against the Hunan Huayue Company in court.

The situation was getting more and more serious. The copycat company was constantly encroaching on the market of Lao Gan Ma at lower prices. The Guizhou company that cooperated with it also began to counterfeit Lao Gan Ma products and blatantly committed infringement.

Products above Everything

The Essence of a Long-Standing Foundation

—Chapter Seven—

Confronting the Copycats

More than once, Tao said she would take the trademark back, even if it would cost her all her fortune. So, the company hired a lawyer and began to collect evidence for suing the Hunan Huayue Company for unfair competition. Tao was confident in this lawsuit. She did not lie about creating the Lao Gan Ma chili sauce; her company had the design patent rights, and she believed in the justice of the government policy and law with strong support from the Industrial and Commercial Department of Guizhou.

Lao Gan Ma's trademark registration process was a long and exhausting marathon. The company first applied for a trademark on August 5, 1996. On October 9 that year, the application was rejected for "lacking prominent features, because *laoganma* is a common name in daily life."

The company applied for the trademark again for the title Lao Gan Ma and for "Tao Huabi and her portrait" in December 1996. On June 21, 1998, the trademark for "Tao Huabi and her portrait" was approved for registration, while the one for Lao Gan Ma was rejected.

On April 13, 1998, the company applied for the trademark for Lao Gan Ma for the third time. It was processed on April 16 but rejected on January 6, 1999, for the same reason, "lacking prominent features, because *laoganma* is a common name in daily life."

The fourth time, in October 1998, the application for trademark registration "Tao Huabi Lao Gan Ma and Portrait" was accepted.

The fifth time, on December 30, 1998, the application for trademark registration "Tao Huabi Lao Gan Ma and Pictures" was accepted.

The lawyer told Tao that among the five applications, except for the fourth application in the 29th category of commodities, which refers to meat products, vegetables, and other horticultural foods for daily use or storage, the rest were all applied in the 30th category of commodities, or plant-derived foods for daily use or storage, and seasonings, etc. The case was reviewed after the third application was rejected, but it was eventually turned down.

Starting from December 1, 1998, Hunan Lao Gan Ma applied to the Trademark Office for trademark registration of "Liu Xiangqiu Lao Gan Ma and Pictures," which was accepted and announced.

On May 14, 2000, when "Liu Xiangqiu Lao Gan Ma and Pictures" of Hunan Huayue Company was registered as a trademark in the 29th category of commodities, it indicated that *laoganma* was no longer a common name in daily life and acknowledged by the Trademark Office. The lawyer believed that the registration was obtained through unfair means and was prepared to request the office to revoke it in accordance with the provisions of the Trademark Law Dispute Ruling.

The media also compared the health batch number [96] No. 000859 of Guiyang Lao Gan Ma with the Hunan Lao Gan Ma [97] No. 0745, proving that Guiyang Lao Gan Ma existed first. After the Lao Gan Ma company in Hunan started production, the Fair-Trade Office of the Guizhou Provincial Administration for Industry and Commerce specifically sent a letter to the Hunan Provincial Administration for Industry and Commerce in November 1997. The two parties worked together to investigate the Hunan Lao Gan Ma company in accordance with the Anti-Unfair Competition Law.

Nevertheless, the reality was that the Hunan company already had a trademark, and it was processed even prior to that of Tao's company. On November 30, 1999, Lao Gan Ma took Hunan Huayue Company to court on the grounds of unfair competition.

During this marathon-like process, Tao received more and more complaints. After the Hubei dealer told her about Hunan Lao Gan Ma products appearing in the local area, some consumers also wrote to report that many Hunan Lao Gan Ma products appeared in the Wuhan market. One consumer, who was a lawyer, wrote in a letter that the Hunan products were very similar to the authentic Lao Gan Ma products in terms of color, shape, food packaging pattern, etc., and sold at a lower price. Consumers must take pains to identify the subtle differences, and it was natural to assume the two companies belonged to the same investor.

"I went to Changsha on a business trip and discovered the same issue. I realized that the other party violated the Anti-Unfair Competition Law and was an infringing product. I hereby report it and suggest that this lawsuit be filed in Wuhan, the place of infringement, rather than in Changsha, to avoid local protectionism," another consumer named Tian from Hunan wrote. He said that he wanted to buy Tao's product but ended up buying the wrong one, which was poorly made. He checked the packaging carefully and saw "Lao **Da** Ma" on the label instead of "Lao **Gan** Ma." He said that such products would not only damage consumers' interests but also harm Lao Gan Ma's reputation.

Hearing this, Tao felt grateful for her loyal customers, and she knew she must keep fighting for her company and for herself. She believed that the state would protect the reasonable demands of the legitimate operation of enterprises.

In June 1999, the Industrial and Commercial Department of Nanming District, Guiyang City, cooperated with the local department in Xi'an in cracking down on counterfeiting and investigated a food factory in Nanming, Guiyang, that had cooperated with the Hunan Lao Gan Ma company.

When asked why his packaging bottle stickers were similar to those of Lao Gan Ma, Mr. Meng, the person in charge of this food factory, replied that he imitated Lao Gan Ma's packaging because it looked good. He also admitted that he had produced more than 1,000 packages, each containing 24 bottles. If each bottle was sold at 8 *yuan*, consumers would have spent nearly 200,000 *yuan* in mistaken purchases.

Tao was very angry when she first learned about Meng's production. At this point, she understood that this copycat company had long been planning to seize the fruits of her hard work.

A Compassionate Heart with Decisive Actions

When collecting evidence, the lawyer found a breakthrough from a former partner of the Hunan Lao Gan Ma company and obtained a confession from the person responsible for the food factory, Meng.

Meng came to know the legal representative of Hunan Lao Gan Ma, Yi, and others when he went to Changsha to promote his chili oil products. Yi initially wanted to use Meng's products in the Hunan sales market, but he was not satisfied with the brand "Ye Lang Nü." He presented Meng with some bottles and trademark designs, and the latter recognized them as Lao Gan Ma's. Yi ignored Meng's hesitation and insisted on plagiarizing Lao Gan Ma's packaging, saying, "You won't be responsible for anything."

With part of his funds already invested at that point, Meng had no choice but to sign the contract with Yi to jointly produce the Lao Gan Ma series of products with Hunan Huayue Company on the condition of providing production technology. Later, after their contract was terminated, Meng opened the Xi'an Sanjiazhuang branch of Guiyang Nanming Tangmeng Food Factory and continued to produce Lao Gan Ma flavored black bean chili sauce and other products.

Lao Gan Ma filed a lawsuit in the Beijing No. 2 Intermediate People's Court, accusing Hunan Huayue Company and Beijing Wangjing Shopping Center of selling their products that infringed on its legitimate rights and interests. It requested the termination of all infringement action, the destruction of all infringing logos, a public apology from Hunan Huayue Company, and a compensation fee of 400,000 *yuan* for its economic losses.

On August 10, 2000, the court officially issued a verdict. The judgment stated, "It is easy to see from the history of the plaintiff Lao Gan Ma Company that *laoganma*, as an honorific for the company's founder, Ms. Tao Huabi, and as a trade name, has been closely associated with the company and the flavored black bean sauce it produces. The label design of the flavored black bean packaging bottle used by the Lao Gan Ma Company has a certain degree of originality and should also be protected."

The judgment also stated, "The defendant company produces and sells the same product as the plaintiff Lao Gan Ma Company—flavored black bean sauce. The former lacks a reasonable basis and has the obvious intention to 'hitchhike.' The products of the defendant company that were produced with the Guiyang Nanming Tangmeng Food Factory from November 1997 to early 1998 were very similar to that of Lao

Gan Ma Company in terms of pattern design, color, content, text, etc. The bottle stickers used on the tempeh packaging bottles are identical, and even the unique font of the three characters of the plaintiff, 'Lao Gan Ma,' is the same. Therefore, the above behavior of the defendant company constitutes unfair competition. The defendant company should bear corresponding legal responsibility for this."

The court held that Hunan Huayue Company's bottle stickers that obtained the design patent had "no substantial changes" compared with the original bottle stickers copied from Lao Gan Ma Company. However, in its reply, Hunan Lao Gan Ma claimed that "the plaintiff has not registered the name 'Lao Gan Ma' and therefore does not enjoy the exclusive right to use the trademark."

Tao's lawyer argued that the Trademark Office's refusal to register the "Lao Gan Ma" trademark has objectively played a role in "protecting" the Hunan company's counterfeiting and infringement. On December 1, 1998, Hunan Huayue Company submitted a trademark registration application for "Liu Xiangqiu Lao Gan Ma and Pictures" to the Trademark Office and was approved, indicating that the title *laoganma* was no longer considered as "lacking distinctive features." The office granted the Hunan company's "Liu Xiangqiu Lao Gan Ma and Pictures" trademark the preliminary review approval, whereas Guiyang Lao Gan Ma's application was only approved for registration after several rejections.

It was not until August 3, 2000, a few days before the trial, that the Trademark Office officially made a ruling and approved both companies' trademarks on the grounds that the two "can be clearly distinguished and will not be easily confused and misidentified."

This decision of the Trademark Office not only became the excuse for Hunan Huayue Company to defend its behavior in court but also affected the relevant court proceedings.

The Beijing No. 2 Intermediate People's Court confirmed the infringement facts of Hunan Huayue Company. Its final judgment was Hunan Huayue Company must stop using and destroy its unused infringed bottle stickers. It must compensate for Lao Gan Ma's economic losses of 150,000 *yuan* before obtaining the design patent. However, it did not support Lao Gan Ma Company's other claims since "in view that the Trademark Office has approved the registration of the defendant's trademark 'Liu Xiangqiu Lao Gan Ma and Pictures.'"

Now, the issue was made complicated again.

"Bone-Scratching" Crackdown on the Counterfeit Products

T he court's judgment implied that the Hunan Lao Gan Ma must compensate for its previous illegal gains, but the two Lao Gan Ma brands could coexist in the future. This case involved laws regarding trademarks, anti-unfair competition, patents, etc. Tao asked the lawyers to find her the corresponding laws and read them to her one by one.

In February 1993, China's revised Trademark Law stipulated that words, graphics, or combinations used in trademarks should have distinctive features and be easily identified. If two or more applicants apply for registration of the same or similar trademark on the same or similar goods, the trademark that was applied for first will be preliminarily reviewed and announced; if the application is made on the same day, the trademark applied first will be preliminarily reviewed and announced for use. For an earlier trademark, applications from others will be rejected and will not be announced. The trademark registration application date shall be when the Trademark Office receives the application documents. If the application procedures are incomplete or the application documents are not filled in as required, the application will be returned, and the application date will not be retained.

The Anti-Unfair Competition Law promulgated in September 1993 defined unfair competition as follows: unauthorized use of the unique names, packaging, and decoration of well-known commodities, or use of names, packaging, and decoration similar to those of well-known commodities, resulting in confusion with other people's well-known goods, causing buyers to mistake them for the well-known goods.

China's revised Patent Law promulgated in September 1992 stipulated that the design for which a patent right is granted shall be different or not similar to the design publicly published in domestic and foreign publications or publicly used at home and abroad before the filing date.

Based on such legal evidence, Lao Gan Ma Company decided to file an appeal again. It was unacceptable for Tao to share her self-made brand with an infringer, and it was ridiculous that she should do so, especially after the court had already acknowledged her rights as the sole original owner of Lao Gan Ma chili sauce.

The case attracted attention from domestic media such as *China Youth Daily* and *Economic Information Daily*. In her interview with the *China Youth Daily*, Tao said that based on the court's judgment, the investigation by the Industrial and Commercial Department, and consumer complaints, Hunan Huayue Company started by counterfeiting well-known products. If such products were allowed to operate under the name of other brands and designs, it would be disrespectful to the protection of the normal competitive order of the market economy, irresponsible to consumers, and contempt for intellectual property rights. If Hunan Huayue Company's trademark registration was allowed, could other counterfeit products also be registered?

Tao also told the reporters that if *laoganma* could not be registered as a commonplace title for ordinary people, why could similar titles such as *kangshifu* (Master Kang), *hongdama* (Aunt Hong), and *guifuren* (Her Ladyship) be approved? Why could both companies named *laoganma* register now? This was actively supporting illegal and unfair competition. Trademarks should be exclusively unique, and their registration should be handled strictly in accordance with the law, following the principles of first-to-application and first-to-use.

An Underregulated Market

I n its appeal to the Beijing Higher People's Court, Lao Gan Ma Company cited the Reply on How to Handle Issues in Patent Infringement Litigation Where All Parties Own Patent Rights issued by the High People's Court on August 16, 1993. The Reply stated, "The People's Court should not reject the plaintiff's lawsuit simply on the grounds that the defendant owns the patent rights without analyzing and judging whether it constitutes patent infringement. Instead, it should analyze the specific circumstances of the defendant's patent ownership and its relationship to the plaintiff's patent to determine whether it constitutes infringement."

Therefore, after comparing the two bottle stickers, the court had already confirmed that the two designs had no substantial differences except for the shape of the portrait frame, so it should make an infringement judgment.

A few days later, Tao learned from a newspaper that the Hunan Lao Gan Ma Company stated in the media that they were also victims of the case. Mr. Li, deputy general manager of the Hunan Huayue Company, said in the newspaper, "The Trademark Office approved our trademark registration on December 1, 1998, and the Guiyang Lao Gan Ma Company was approved later than ours on December 30 the same year. In the Trademark Office's preliminary announcement, our trademark registration was on December 30, 1999, and the Guiyang Lao Gan Ma Company's trademark registration was on January 7, 2000. Both our trademark approval and announcement came first. Therefore, Hunan Huayue Company should have priority."

Under such instigation, Makro removed all Tao's products from its three supermarkets and replaced them with Hunan Huayue Company's products. The company also went to some supermarkets to hang up banners to promote their brand and products.

To recover Lao Gan Ma's trademark, Tao and some leaders of Guizhou Province proactively sought support from the State Administration for Market Regulation, but the answer they received was that both companies could use the Lao Gan Ma trademark.

Facing various pressures, Tao remained undeterred. "I don't care how powerful my enemies are. Power does not mean they can be unreasonable. Our country promotes fair trade, and the law will never allow them to act recklessly. I will fight this lawsuit even if it costs everything I have. I respect anyone who can create their own brand, but if they think they can copy or rob my brand, then they think wrong. What is mine will always be mine, and I am not afraid of them."

During that time, Tao received much help from local government leaders at all levels. Sun Guoqiang, then mayor of Guiyang, and Long Yongtu, chief negotiator for China's accession to the World Trade Organization (WTO), provided help to Guiyang Lao Gan Ma and greatly improved the debate level of the Lao Gan Ma litigation team.

Truth and Fame

Tao entrusted An Xiang, a trademark attorney of Zhongyuan Xinda Intellectual Property Agency Co., Ltd., and Zou Hailin, a lawyer at Kehua Law Firm, to defend her case in the trial. On March 20, 2001, the Beijing Higher People's Court issued the final penalty. Hunan Lao Gan Ma constituted unfair competition. It must stop using the title "Lao Gan Ma" when producing flavored black bean products, stop using bottle stickers similar to Lao Gan Ma's, compensate for economic losses of 400,000 *yuan*, and publish an apology in the newspaper. Finally, Guiyang Lao Gan Ma won the lawsuit and recovered its brand. "This is the final verdict. They cannot appeal again according to legal procedures," said Zou. Hearing this, Tao almost burst into tears for the hard-earned victory.

The verdict stated, "The Beijing Higher People's Court has confirmed that the Shihui Restaurant in Guiyang was established in January 1994 by Ms. Tao Huabi. The restaurant was renamed Guiyang Nanming Tao's Flavor Food Store in November 1994, Guiyang Nanming Tao's Flavor Food Factory in May 1997, and Guiyang Nanming Lao Gan Ma Flavor Food Co., Ltd. in November 1997. In November 1994, Guiyang Lao Gan Ma Company launched flavored foods under the title 'Lao Gan Ma.' Among them, Lao Gan Ma flavored soybeans were highly popular among consumers."

The verdict also illustrated that in August 1996, Guiyang Nanming Tao's Flavor Food Store began to use bottle stickers designed by its manager, Li Guishan. The basic color of the stickers was red, with a portrait of the product inventor, Ms. Tao Huabi, in the middle. On the lower part of the portrait were the characters, *laoganma*, in a distinctive font. On the left and right sides of the portrait were the words "Shihui Restaurant" and "flavored soybeans" written in yellow oval frames. The product description was written on the left, and the formula and execution standards were written on the right. Above and below these texts were the words "fragrant and spicy," "elegant and exquisite," "Guizhou specialty," and "high quality." Each character was contained in yellow oval circles.

In December 1997, Li Guishan applied for a design patent to the Patent Office for the Lao Gan Ma package design and obtained the patent right on August 22, 1998. Li also registered for the copyright of the product design with the Guizhou Provincial Copyright Bureau on December 30, 1997. In January 1999, the Guiyang Municipal People's Government listed Lao Gan Ma flavored soybeans as a famous brand product in Guiyang. The Guizhou Provincial Economic and Trade Commission and the Guizhou Provincial Technical Supervision Bureau confirmed Tao's Lao Gan Ma flavored soybeans as a famous brand product in Guizhou Province. In November 1999, the China National Food Industry Association awarded Lao Gan Ma Company the Advanced Enterprise Certificate. Lao Gan Ma Company provided relevant evidence on the quantity of Lao Gan Ma flavored food it sold each year from 1997 to 2000 and its tax payment to the state, proving that its sales in 1998 were 45.48 million *yuan* and it paid 3.29 million *yuan* in taxes. The sales in 1999 were 107 million *yuan*, and the company paid nearly 15 million *yuan* in taxes; the sales in 2000 were

131.5 million *yuan*, and the company paid 24.64 million *yuan* in taxes.

On the other side, Hunan Huayue Company was established in September 1997. In November of the same year, the company signed a Joint Venture Agreement with Guiyang Nanming Tangmeng Food Factory, agreeing that both parties would jointly develop and produce Lao Gan Ma flavored soybeans, with Guiyang Nanming Tangmeng Food Factory providing technology and Hunan Huayue Company providing production facilities, required equipment, facilities, and venues. In November 2007, the Lao Gan Ma flavored soybeans jointly produced by the two parties began to go on the market. Compared with Tao's packaging bottle label, Hunan Nanyue Company's packaging was close to identical, only different in its product information, including batch number, implementation standard, manufacturer, factory address, telephone number, and postal code, and Ms. Tao Huabi's portrait. The title "Lao Gan Ma" was excerpted from the calligrapher Mr. Shi Mu's inscription, "Wishing Hunan Lao Gan Ma flavored soybeans a prosperous future." However, in his testimony, Mr. Shi Mu claimed that the three characters in the inscription were copied from the font provided by Hunan Huayue Company and not his own work.

The Beijing Higher People's Court defined "well-known commodities" as commodities with a certain market reputation and were known to the relevant public. Lao Gan Ma flavored food has been favored by consumers ever since it was put on the market and has achieved significant success in a short period. Its sales volume has been on an upward trend despite the impact of infringing products, and the company has paid tens of millions of *yuan* in taxes to the state. Due to the high quality and high reputation of its products, many counterfeit manufacturers have appeared in various places and seriously damaged consumers' interests. In 1998 and 1999, the Guiyang Municipal Administration for Industry and Commerce issued official letters to Industrial and Commercial Administration Bureaus across the country many times requesting an investigation. Lao Gan Ma's chili sauce should be deemed a "well-known commodity" since the product has a certain market reputation and is a product known to the relevant public.

The Beijing Higher People's Court held that the principle of determining target damage in China's anti-non-application compensation law was that the loss suffered by the rights holder due to the infringing behavior or the benefits obtained by the infringer shall be the compensation for damage. Because Lao

Gan Ma did not provide the losses it suffered caused by the infringement, and Hunan Huayue Company did not provide the profits it gained, the court made its decision based on the actual situation. Hunan Huayue Company spent nearly 1.6 million *yuan* advertising its products from 1998 to 1999. According to business practices, profits earned by operators were usually higher than advertising investment, so Lao Gan Ma requested a compensation of 400,000 *yuan*. It also requested Beijing Yansha Wangjing Shopping Center to stop selling the products involved in the case produced by Hunan Huayue Company. These claims were both deemed legitimate and supported by the court.

Finally, the Higher Court held that the original judgment of the Beijing No. 2 Intermediate People's Court was untenable and should be revised; the grounds for the appeal of Lao Gan Ma Company should be supported; and the grounds for the appeal of Hunan Huayue Company were untenable and should be rejected.

In accordance with Article 2, Paragraph 1, and Article 5, Paragraph 1, Item 2 of the Anti-Unfair Competition Law of the People's Republic of China, as well as Article 153, Paragraph 1, Item 3 of the Civil Procedure Law of the People's Republic of China, the judgment of the case was as follows:

1. Revoke the No. 132 Civil Judgment of the Beijing No. 2 Intermediate People's Court (1999).

2. Hunan Huayue Food Co., Ltd. must stop using the Lao Gan Ma trade name on flavored soybean products.

3. Hunan Huayue Food Co., Ltd. must stop using bottle stickers similar to the Lao Gan Ma flavored soybean bottle stickers produced by Guiyang Nanming Lao Gan Ma Flavor Food Co., Ltd.

4. Hunan Huayue Food Co., Ltd. shall compensate Guiyang Nanming Lao Gan Ma Flavor Food Co., Ltd. for economic losses of 400,000 *yuan* (to be paid within one month after this judgment takes effect).

5. Beijing Yansha Wangjing Shopping Center must stop selling the Lao Gan Ma flavored soybeans produced by Hunan Huayue Food Co., Ltd.

6. Hunan Huayue Food Co., Ltd. shall apologize to Guiyang Nanming Lao Gan Ma Flavor Food Co., Ltd. in a nationally circulated newspaper within one month after this judgment takes effect.

Applause sounded after the verdict was announced in court. Tao had finally completed the protection of her rights.

Word-of-Mouth Economy

Building Core Competitiveness

-Chapter Eight-

Lao Gan Ma and Lao Gan Die

After Lao Gan Ma won the trademark battle, Tao successfully registered a trademark for her company. This case was rated one of the "Top Ten Classic Cases of Intellectual Property" by the Beijing Higher People's Court. Both Tao's determination to safeguard the Lao Gan Ma brand and the consequence of counterfeiting were known to the public. More importantly, Lao Gan Ma received legal protection for its future operation.

But problems arose again. After Lao Gan Ma received its title, more products titled "Gan" appeared, such as Lao Gan Die (old godfather), Lao Gan Niang (another saying for old godmother), Lao Tai Po (old lady), Gan Er Zi (godson), as well as Sichuan Gan Ma, Yunnan Gan Ma, Southern Sichuan Gan Ma, etc. Tao's journey of cracking down on counterfeiting thus continued. Many of these products were unqualified in their sanitary standards, which not only harmed Lao Gan Ma's reputation but also endangered the health of consumers.

After the lawsuit with Hunan Lao Gan Ma, in Guiyang, a new chili brand was released called Lao Gan Die (old godfather). This brand imitated Lao Gan Ma products in packaging and marketing, even the placement in supermarkets.

Tao immediately submitted a report to the Guizhou Provincial People's Government, suing this company for using Lao Gan Ma's reputation to market their product. However, after many mediations, Lao Gan Die still survived.

For a while, the impression of bundled sales that Lao Gan Die intentionally created by placing its products next to Lao Gan Ma's made people believe that Lao Gan Die was a product under Lao Gan Ma. However, these two types of chili sauces that looked very similar had nothing to do with each other.

This kind of "marketing method" that deliberately confused consumers was a disguised form of infringement. Such an approach was untenable in the market, and it was difficult to maintain long-term operations.

Time has proved that Lao Gan Ma has become a national brand, and its recognition could not be so easily influenced by copycat brands anymore. It has also proved that Tao's concerns when Lao Gan Die first came out were unnecessary because people chose Lao Gan Ma not only because of its reputation but also because of its insistence on quality and trustworthiness to consumers. Based on the rule of preconceptions in business, it would be difficult for any new brand to surpass Lao Gan Ma after the market had already become used to it because consumers tended to judge the quality of all chili sauce products based on Lao Gan Ma's standard. It would be difficult to shake the status of Lao Gan Ma even at several times the price.

Tao's core competitiveness came from the quality of her products. Much attention has been paid to the materials, ingredients, craftsmanship, and the universality of public taste. Some brands used the name Lao Gan Ma in an attempt to raise their own brand standards. Still, lacking a solid foundation in quality building and management, these brands eventually fell apart like "a castle in the air" that could not withstand any practical testing.

An Apology Letter from Haidilao Hot Pot

Tao increased her company's investment in combating counterfeiting every year, and she offered big awards to dealers for cracking down on counterfeiting.

Once, a Shaanxi distributor of Lao Gan Ma Company went to Haidilao Hot Pot with friends. They found the Lao Gan Ma chili sauce provided by the store strange, so they asked the store for an explanation. The store insisted that they used Lao Gan Ma's black bean chili sauce, which was provided in bags.

The distributor, who was very familiar with Lao Gan Ma products, was convinced that these were counterfeit products because Lao Gan Ma had never packed its products in bags. He called the "City Express" program of Shaanxi Radio and Television Station, and the reporting team of the program exposed the hot pot restaurant through investigation and evidence collection. Later, the restaurant explained that they had put the wrong stickers on the bags and immediately replaced the Lao Gan Ma stickers with the ones that read "flavored black bean sauce."

After receiving the dealer's report on this incident, Lao Gan Ma Company immediately entrusted him with full authority to handle the matter. Later, Haidilao released the "Apology Letter Regarding the Infringement of Black Bean Chili Sauce Labeled as Lao Gan Ma" through the Internet. The letter wrote: "The regional agent of the Lao Gan Ma Company has complained about the infringement of certain stores of our company in Xi'an by labeling certain black bean chili sauce as Lao Gan Ma's product. After the incident, we immediately investigated the company and found that some stores had indeed mislabeled the chili sauces they used. These sauces, provided by qualified manufacturers, were incorrectly labeled as Lao Gan Ma's."

"We are deeply aware that this incident has exposed our weak awareness of trademark rights and low and irregular management levels, and it has harmed the interests of a company well received by the public and highly respected by us."

Haidilao sincerely apologized to Lao Gan Ma Company and consumers, and it promised to actively assume all responsibilities, including legal liabilities.

Usually, many companies were afraid of counterfeiting. They believed that it would cause consumers to lose faith in the brand and thus affect sales. But Tao was not afraid. The Lao Gan Ma Company has a budget for special anti-counterfeiting actions every year and will immediately crack down on counterfeit goods if found, with zero tolerance.

When a counterfeit product was identified, the first thing to do was to issue a solemn statement telling everyone that Lao Gan Ma had never commissioned other companies to produce its products, nor had it cooperated with any company in any way. Then, a special anti-counterfeiting team was set up to knock down the counterfeiters one by one. The company would also work with relevant government departments, such as the Industrial and Commercial Departments of Guiyang City and Nanming District.

Creating an Industry

T he battle against the Hunan Huayue Company made Lao Gan Ma even more popular. Many media began to pay attention to Tao's story. In 2006, Tao was interviewed by Xiao Lu, a reporter from the magazine *Contemporary Guizhou*, and the article "Tao Huabi: Three Firsts, Four Wishes" written after the interview was one of the few resources of Tao's oral history compiled by reporters after she became a legend.

This interview took place after the Guizhou Province implemented the Guizhou Provincial People's Government's Opinions on Implementing Several Opinions of the State Council on Encouraging, Supporting, and Guiding the Development of Non-public Economic Development Such as Individual Businesses in 2006. The Opinions contained 42 articles, with "equality" and "equal treatment" being keywords. The development of Guizhou's non-public economy has received greater policy support. In the same year, Lao Gan Ma oil chili pepper sauce obtained the title of "Chinese Famous Brand Product."

"Many years ago, a reporter told me, '*Laoganma*, you are not just selling chili peppers; you are creating an industry in China.' I didn't understand it at the time, but now I admire the vision of these media friends. We had great news in September. Lao Gan

Ma was rated as a famous Chinese brand product, the first in the country's chili products industry, the first in Guizhou's food industry, and the first among Guizhou's non-public enterprises. I am very happy to have won three first places in one year. This year, the National Standard for Oil Chili Peppers based on our production and operation has been released and implemented nationwide." In the article, Tao shared the happy events for Lao Gan Ma.

She recalled, "2006 was the tenth year since I founded the company. More than twenty years ago, when I was selling starch jelly in Longdongbao, my regular customers praised my chili sauce, and they all said that I should just start a special chili company. I feel very emotional thinking these old days. Now, I don't have to worry about the company's year-end summary, but I want to make a few wishes for the first ten years of Lao Gan Ma—I hope that the burden on employees will be less, that the company will have more talents, that there will be fewer infringements, and that there will be more good companies."

"The kids in our company are very close to me. They call me Aunt Tao, Mom, or *laoganma*. Very few people call me chairman. I am used to going to the factory every day to check each workshop. If I don't smell the chili pepper, I will feel uncomfortable all over.

When I am free, I chat with everyone. Most of the company's grassroots employees came from rural areas of Guizhou, Hunan, and Sichuan. These children, far away from their parents, love to chat with me about their worries, joys, and difficulties. I have always used one standard to measure everything and everyone. For all regular employees, I provide them with the "three insurances."* Over time, they are like my own children. I praise them for their good performances and scold them for bad ones. I believe that if I treat them with my heart, they will also repay me with their love," said Tao.

Regarding talents, Tao shared that the company's rule for employment was to "be a good person first before doing great things." "Many people said, 'Lao Gan Ma has a group of very capable young people.' I feel very pleased to hear this. I am not educated, but I know one thing: be a good person before doing great things. Even those college graduates in my company agreed with me. I think the ability level may affect the company's decision-making level for a period of time, but character defects will bring long-term negative effects. There are many excellent college graduates who expressed their willingness to come to Lao

---

* Pension insurance, basic medical insurance, and unemployment insurance.

Gan Ma to find a job and start a business. They recognized my brand; how could I not live up to their trust? But I don't want people with big names who are not honest. I would rather find someone who is willing to learn and work hard. I am an upright person, so I also help upright people."

When asked about infringement, Tao said that if a tree grew big, it would attract the wind. The brand and reputation she had worked so hard to build were now regarded as an easy target by various companies. In 2006, the General Administration of Quality Supervision, Inspection, and Quarantine sent personnel to teach Lao Gan Ma how to combat counterfeiting. Therefore, the company specially organized a group of business experts to go to various parts of the country to crack down on chili sauce products such as Lao Gan Ba, Lao Gan Niang, and Gan Er Zi, which were particularly similar in packaging to Lao Gan Ma.

She said, "People who know me well know that I have a short temper, but I am very straightforward and down-to-earth. Whether I was selling starch jelly at a stall or running a business of today's scale, I have always been honest, never sold fake products or evaded taxes. So, I especially hate those who step on other people's shoulders and want to take shortcuts."

Tao wished that there were more profitable enterprises in Guizhou. She revealed that in the past few years, when the company had just ended its infringement lawsuit and was gradually getting on the right track, the leaders from a certain city in Hubei came to Longdongbao to see her five or six times a year to encourage Lao Gan Ma to relocate to Hubei. They also said that the railway would directly connect to the company's factory base and provide them with all preferential policies and tax conditions. Tao said she could feel the sincerity of these leaders, but she started her factory in Nanming District, Guiyang City, Guizhou Province. Therefore, she declined the offer. Some people said she was being silly, but she was very serious.

In 2006, Lao Gan Ma Company developed some new products, such as spicy vegetables and fermented peppers. This has led to their increasing demand for raw materials and higher quality requirements. The raw materials such as soybeans, rapeseed oil, and dried peppers purchased in large quantities not only relied on nature but also on the people who received and purchased the goods for the best quality. If any mistake was made with the raw materials, the taste of Lao Gan Ma would change, and the brand would be ruined.

"Comrade Yuan Zhou (then mayor of Guiyang) came to see me one day and said that he saw a Taiwanese travel program introducing Japan. In a shot for a few seconds, there were the words 'Lao Gan Ma Chili Shop' in large characters. He said he was extremely excited to see our brand being so well-known abroad. I want to thank our country leaders for their devotion to the Lao Gan Ma enterprise. It means that we have a greater responsibility now."

"This year is about to pass, and I am thinking of all the government leaders and media friends who helped us during the most difficult period of Lao Gan Ma. They helped us selflessly without asking for anything as a reward. I will always remember my debt to them."

This was the first and only time that Tao told her story in public media.

Redefining the Market with Integrity

Over the years, with the state's strong support for private enterprises and the improvement of intellectual property rights, Lao Gan Ma's anti-counterfeiting efforts have been well protected by local industrial and commercial departments.

In early September 2013, Lao Gan Ma received news that the trademarks used on the bottles of three companies producing black bean chili peppers in Meishan, Sichuan, were almost identical to its own. The anti-counterfeiting personnel of the company reported the case to the Industrial and Commercial Bureau of Nanming District, Guiyang City. After receiving the report, the Bureau immediately organized law enforcement personnel to go to Meishan, Sichuan, to conduct a careful analysis of the three companies' products. After obtaining sufficient evidence, they finally confirmed their infringement.

The Nanming District Industrial and Commercial Bureau formed a task force to go to Meishan to crack down on counterfeiting. With the cooperation of the local industrial and commercial department, they confiscated more than 17,000 "Jiaxiang Lao Gan Ma" logos and more than 70 finished products, each consisting of 24 bottles in the first company alone. In total, more than 100,000 logos and more than 1,000 finished products that infringed on the Lao Gan Ma brand trademark were confiscated, saving tens of millions of *yuan* in direct economic losses for the Lao Gan Ma Company.

In 2016, Lao Gan Ma discovered that a local food company in Guizhou was suspected of infringing on its trademark and immediately filed a lawsuit with the court. What Tao didn't understand was why this company would infringe upon hers since both companies' trademarks were well-known nationally.

Lao Gan Ma's trademark was approved for registration on May 21, 2003. The approved products were in the 30th category, including soybeans, chili sauce (seasoning), fried oil chili, etc. The Lao Gan Ma trademark has been recognized as a well-known trademark by the Trademark Office and other departments many times in 2011, 2014, 2015, and 2016. The other food company owned a series of registered trademarks called "Niutou Brand and Pictures," and its products were approved as the 29th category (beef products). The "Niutou Brand and Pictures" trademark was recognized as a well-known trademark by the Trademark Office in 2010.

In February 2016, the marketing department of Lao Gan Ma discovered that Beijing Carrefour Company's branch store at Ciyun Temple was selling products labeled "Niutou Brand Lao Gan Ma Beef Sticks." The upper front of the packaging was marked with the "Niutou Brand and Pictures" trademark, and the words "Lao Gan Ma" were printed in the middle.

Lao Gan Ma believed that the Guizhou food company and Beijing Carrefour Company had infringed on its exclusive right to use well-known trademarks, so it brought the case to the Beijing Intellectual Property Court and requested the Guizhou company and Beijing Carrefour Company to immediately cease such behavior, a compensation fee for Lao Gan Ma's economic losses of eight million *yuan* and reasonable expenses of 124,500 *yuan* for the case.

In court, the Guizhou food company argued that using the words "Lao Gan Ma" on the products' packaging was a reasonable indication to disclose that the products had truly been added with Lao Gan Ma chili sauce. The distinctiveness and recognition of the Lao Gan Ma trademark would not be diluted. They also believed that their company and Lao Gan Ma belonged to different industries and would not squeeze the original consumer market of Lao Gan Ma. The behavior involved in the case did not belong to identifying trademarks and would not cause consumers to confuse the source of the goods.

The first instance hearing of the Beijing Intellectual Property Court held that the defendant company's behavior of adding the words "Lao Gan Ma" on the packaging of the goods involved in the case caused consumers to mistakenly believe that the company had certain connections with Lao Gan Ma. This behavior clearly identified the origin of the goods, making it a trademark use and not falling within the scope of fair use.

Finally, the Beijing Intellectual Property Court ruled that the Guizhou food company should immediately stop using the words "Lao Gan Ma" on its beef stick products, and Beijing Carrefour Company should stop selling these products with the words "Lao Gan Ma" printed on them.

The court did not support Lao Gan Ma's request for economic loss compensation of eight million *yuan*. It held that neither party had provided sufficient evidence to prove the actual losses or benefits gained due to the infringement involved in the case, and it was difficult to determine the registered trademark license fee. Therefore, considering the degree of subjective fault of the Guizhou food company, its business operations, the nature, scope, consequences of the infringement, the reputation of the well-known trademark, and other factors, the court determined at its discretion the amount that the Guizhou food company should compensate Lao Gan Ma Company in total was 150,000 *yuan*.

Both parties were dissatisfied with this verdict and appealed to the Beijing Higher People's Court.

On May 16, 2016, the Beijing Higher People's Court made a final judgment that recognized the Guizhou food company's infringement of Lao Gan Ma's trademark but still did not support Lao Gan Ma's request for compensation for economic losses. It changed the first-instance compensation amount to 175,000 *yuan* and rejected the other appeals of both parties.

In addition, Lao Gan Ma claimed three million *yuan* in economic losses and reasonable expenses from the defendant company on the grounds of trademark infringement. In April 2017, the final judgment upheld the first-instance judgment and ordered the defendant to compensate Lao Gan Ma for economic losses and reasonable expenses of 426,500 *yuan*. This meant that Lao Gan Ma claimed a total of 11 million *yuan* from the defendant company for trademark infringement and finally received a compensation of 601,500 *yuan*.

At the Two Sessions,* Tao submitted a proposal on "cracking down on counterfeiting." She believed that cracking down on counterfeiting was related to the economic order of the entire country.

Some media outlets reported on her issue, and one of them wrote a review titled "Learn from Lao Gan Ma on Zero

---

* The Two Sessions is the collective term for the Chinese government's annual plenary sessions of the National People's Congress (NPC) and of the Chinese People's Political Consultative Conference (CPPCC).

Tolerance in Fighting Counterfeiting." It believed that as long as the government, enterprises, and consumers work together, counterfeiters would find it difficult to survive in a limited space. For the government, it was necessary to improve laws and regulations, implement the responsibilities for combating counterfeiting, and ensure that those who crack down on counterfeiting had legal support. Enterprises should correct their past mentality of not being able to crack down on counterfeiting or to speak out about counterfeiting. Although it seemed time-consuming, laborious, and expensive, cracking down on counterfeiting was the only way for enterprises to develop. For consumers, not buying fake products and reporting them to relevant departments was the simplest but most sufficient help.

Fine Management

The Trivial
and the
Detailed

—Chapter Nine—

Lao Gan Ma's Down-to-Earth Management Method

Many people wondered how Tao managed her fast-expanding company with more than 6,000 people without international and advanced management tactics. What Tao did was train disciples and work with her employees. "In Guizhou, craftsmen are highly respected," she said. Like carpenters who solemnly offered sacrifices to their ritual ancestor Lu Ban before building houses and blacksmiths who paid homage to the Daoist god Taishang Laojun, frying chili peppers and making soybean sauce also required necessary respect for the skill and process. Tao's understanding of craftsmanship was to not do anything against her conscience and ruin the craft's reputation.

She taught her workers to fry chili peppers as her apprentices, and she treated them as her own family.

The main rule she set at work was "don't be lazy," meaning that employees should pay attention both to quantity and quality. Lao Gan Ma worked out a standard to ensure both quantity and quality of products after years of experience for employees to refer to and follow.

Tao was familiar with most of her employees in the company, and she knew 60%–70% of them by name. Many people thought she had an exceptional memory, but the fact was she dealt with everyone attentively and remembered them by heart. She knew everyone from the company managers to workers and janitors. Lao Gan Ma provided food and accommodation for its employees, but it also had strict requirements. For example, when some of her old employees did not pay attention to hygiene, Tao would straightforwardly remind them. Faced with the question of whether she was being too harsh, Tao replied, "If you can't even do personal hygiene well, how can the food you make be clean and reassuring?"

One year, Lao Gan Ma recruited a lot of college students. One day, not long after they arrived, Tao happened to see a lot of leftover food in the dining hall. The dining hall manager explained that the new employees often did not finish their food, and the person responsible for collecting the leftovers from their dining hall had not been here for the past two days due to some family issues.

Tao detested wasted food more than anything else in her life. These young people could not understand what her generation had experienced during the Great Famine. Some new employees threw away a steamed bun or a bowl of rice after two bites. Angry and sad, Tao went to some of the employees and said,

"You graduated from universities, and yet you don't know how to cherish food? How can you become the pillar of the country in the future? Do you spoiled kids know how many people died because of starvation?"

"We are sorry, *laoganma*. We will never get more than we could eat in the future."

"I'm not saying you should not eat. Of course, you must eat since you are still young. But you must never waste food."

In winter, Tao asked the dining hall to prepare ginger tea for all employees.

Once, when a new employee fell sick, Tao cooked noodles for him and fed them to him in bed. When some others went on a business trip, Tao made them some hard-boiled eggs and saw them off at the train station. "*Laoganma*, are you seeing off your sons?" some asked.

"Yeah, kind of," she answered. Tao allowed these new employees to slowly integrate into the community and get used to life in the company, just like family members.

On her employees' birthdays, Tao bought them gifts and asked the canteen to cook them a bowl of "longevity noodles" with a poached egg in it. When an employee got married, Tao would help out as much as she could, like hosting a banquet in his or her hometown. No matter how busy she was, she always tried to attend the ceremony, give the new couple red envelopes, and be their witness.

There was a widely circulated story about the company's dining hall. A cook from a rural area lost both his parents early on and had to raise two younger brothers by himself. He got into drinking and was drunk all day long. Tao thought that he couldn't continue like this. She prepared a big meal, bought a bottle of good wine, and invited the young cook to dinner. At the dinner table, she said to him, "Son, you can eat and drink as much as you want today, but from tomorrow on, you must stop drinking. Your two brothers are still young, and you must work to send them to school. Don't let them be like me, who doesn't know a single word."

The young cook's eyes welled up in tears and said, "*Ganma*, no one has ever taught me anything since my parents died. I'll listen to you. I will stop drinking and smoking and send my brothers to school."

"I will give you 200 *yuan* every month starting tomorrow," said Tao, "and save the rest of your wages for you. Just come to me whenever you need to pay for your brothers' tuition."

From then on, the young cook was a different man. He never drank again and was more optimistic about life and more diligent. His two younger brothers both got into college and found good jobs after graduation. When they came to visit their elder brother, the latter would say, "Go see *laoganma* first. If it weren't for her, I probably would have already been wasted, and you both wouldn't have had the chance to go to college."

Some management personnel used to persuade Tao to stay out of these trivial matters to avoid bringing unnecessary risks to the company. But to Tao, these were no trivial matters. She wanted to teach these young employees to be good people, to cherish food, and to be diligent and frugal.

No Termites Allowed in the Company

Everything Tao did was done with conscience, and she was willing to do whatever was good for other people's benefit. This made some people think they could take advantage of her generosity and that of the big company. To these people, especially those who held important positions in the company, Tao never hesitated to punish them with legal weapons.

In the past, Tao fully trusted her chili pepper suppliers and did not weigh the materials provided. After some time, thinking Tao was careless and easy to deceive, the suppliers began to give short weight in each bag, putting only 70 or 60 *jin* of peppers when it should have been 80. What they didn't know was that Tao was very sensitive to weight, thanks to her experience selling vegetables. She could measure almost the exact weight of anything just by hand. She thus confronted the supplier and asked for an explanation. When he couldn't, she stopped cooperating with him.

Tao had many relatives in Zunyi who also provided chili peppers for Lao Gan Ma. Despite the small quantity, the company accepted their supplies for old times' sake. Once, an old lady's supplied goods were found to be of poor quality with pebbles in them. Tao was extremely irritated and shouted at the woman in front of everyone. She didn't ask these relatives to cut the pepper roots like she asked the other suppliers, yet they did not appreciate this privilege and continued to exploit her kindness and their relationship. She couldn't imagine what these pebbles would do to her company and reputation if they were not detected before being made into the chili sauce.

Hearing this, the old lady burst into tears and accused Tao of being ungrateful and unkind. But Tao was only following the rules. When Lao Gan Ma was formulating its management regulations, Tao asked not to copy the regulations of other companies but to formulate simple rules such as "don't be lazy at work" and "be honest, don't steal," and the entire company must strictly abide by them.

After the company grew bigger, Tao focused on production quality, and some suppliers took the opportunity to collude with the weighers and steal from the company. For example, the weighers would report 3,000 *jin* of peppers when the suppliers provided only 2,000 and save the money for the extra 1,000 *jin* for themselves.

In 2011, Tao realized something was wrong with the pepper supply, so she asked the security department to investigate it. One day in November 2011, the security department reported that the suspect supplier had come again. The inspectors stopped the cart, weighed it, and found that it was short by several thousand *jin*. They immediately called the police and arrested the supplier and the weigher.

The police discovered that such sneaky action had begun on April 1, 2011. The suppliers and weighers would agree to calculate the truck lighter than its actual weight so that the peppers on the truck would appear heavier on the scale. On that day, the truck's actual weight was 15,260 kilograms, but it was only calculated as 11,810 kilograms. The weight difference was all counted as peppers, and the falsely reported portion reached 3,433.1 kilograms.

Based on the contract price of 17.2 *yuan* per kilogram between the company and the suppliers at that time, this car alone appropriated 59,049 *yuan* from the company. From April to October 2011, 36 such crimes were committed, and more than 1.7 million *yuan* of the company's money was lost.

The court decided that the three defendants, surnamed Fu, Hu, and Long, had illegally appropriated more than 1.7 million *yuan* of property belonging to Lao Gan Ma Company for themselves, and their actions constituted the crime of official embezzlement. According to the provisions of China's criminal law, the defendants Fu, Hu, and Long were sentenced to ten years in prison, deprived of political rights for one year, confiscated 20,000 *yuan*, and had to return the stolen money.

In addition to theft, leaking the company's secrets, such as formulas, was another redline that Lao Gan Ma employees knew they must stay away from. Formulas were very important to food companies. Many people tried to counterfeit Lao Gan Ma products but eventually failed. One of the core reasons was that they did not have Tao's exclusive formula, so the taste they made could not compete against Lao Gan Ma's.

After running Lao Gan Ma for so many years, Tao has dealt with all kinds of competitors, both legitimate and unfair, within and outside the province. In these competitions, she developed strong market monitoring capabilities. The annual anti-counterfeiting funds invested by Lao Gan Ma dealers also played a big role in market monitoring. The company could almost always receive immediate feedback wherever counterfeit products appeared.

Many people refer to Lao Gan Ma's method of cracking down on counterfeiting as "bone-scratching." When counterfeit goods were discovered, Lao Gan Ma would attack them decisively without any ambiguity. Many of Lao Gan Ma's formulas were confidential. Some people even jokingly claimed the formulas were Tao's strongest weapon for dominating the chili sauce world.

Strike the Traitor

The formulas were still leaked one day.

After the company received the information, the management personnel quickly compared the target products with Lao Gan Ma's and realized that they were indeed very similar in taste. It was impossible to develop this formula by oneself without knowing it since it took the company repeated experiments to finalize it.

Not many people had access to this formula, and the company soon found out the suspicious personnel through investigation. "*Langanma*, you must not keep such a traitor!" some employees said.

The company immediately called the police. The company alone could not complete the evidence collection and had to rely on the investigation of the public security organs. After investigation, the Nanming Branch of the Guiyang Municipal Public Security Bureau discovered that someone had indeed illegally leaked the formula of Lao Gan Ma Company.

Investigators purchased suspected products and submitted them to the Judicial Expertise Center. The appraisal result was the target product contained detailed technical information about Lao Gan Ma products, which was not available to the public during manufacturing.

Since the company suspected of stealing the technology has never been involved in this field and thus did not have such research and development capabilities, Lao Gan Ma had also never transferred the manufacturing technology to any company or individual. The police concluded that someone had illegally leaked Lao Gan Ma's formula. The police conducted extensive analysis and investigation and finally identified Mr. Jia, a former Lao Gan Ma employee, as the suspect of committing the crime.

Jia worked at Lao Gan Ma from 2003 to 2015. When he first joined the company, he was a technician in the quality department. He improved very quickly and had strong business capabilities. Later, he became an engineer, and his salary increased from a few thousand *yuan* to tens of thousands of *yuan* per month. Afterward, Lao Gan Ma gave him access to all the company's proprietary technologies, production processes, and other core secret information, including the secret formulas of Lao Gan Ma's flavored soybean sauce.

Of course, Jia signed a confidentiality agreement with Lao Gan Ma based on the company's regulation, which stipulated that Jia must keep the company's business secrets during work and after leaving his job and could not engage in similar or competitive business activities. Later, Jia was fined half a year's wages for violating relevant regulations. Having his salary suddenly deducted by so much was difficult for Jia to accept, and he submitted his resignation, which was approved.

After leaving Lao Gan Ma, Jia was introduced to a small food processing factory in Huaxi with less than ten employees.

He used a fake name and offered to improve the production process of soybean sauce at a controlled price. For more than a year working in the factory, Jia conducted three experiments to improve the formula of Lao Gan Ma and achieved success. Not only did the soybean sauce produced taste similar to that of Lao Gan Ma, but the production cost was about two *yuan* cheaper per bottle.

During the Spring Festival in 2017, Nanming policemen arrested Jia in Guiyang, searched and confiscated his mobile hard drive, and found a lot of information involving Lao Gan Ma's trade secrets in his computer. Jia confessed that in only three months since he was hired at this food factory, the company produced more than 1,000 pieces of soybean products, which were sold in various supermarkets in Guiyang City. He was paid a monthly salary of 7,000 *yuan*.

The police immediately raided the food factory and found that the soybean formula and other information he submitted happened to be the confidential formula of Lao Gan Ma Company. The person in charge of the factory said that after knowing Jia had worked under Tao before coming, he was worried that the professional skills he provided were related to Lao Gan Ma, so he fired Jia. In addition to the more than

1,000 sold products, the rest have been destroyed. Therefore, the police did not detect any modified soybeans.

Police calculated that the amount involved in this major leak case reached tens of millions of *yuan*. On the one hand, similar products were put on the market due to the leakage of the formula. Comparing the sales of the same product of Lao Gan Ma with that of the same period last year, the loss was nearly ten million *yuan* in total; on the other hand, Jia's methods of manually producing secretly improved soybeans in the Huaxi food factory impacted the market for similar products and limited the production efficiency of Lao Gan Ma's special production equipment during this period, resulting in a loss of millions of *yuan*.

In the end, Jia was criminally detained by the police on suspicion of infringement of trade secrets. Tao treated her employees with love and affection, making them feel at home. She was like a Boddhisattva with people worthy of her trust, but she was like thunder with those who crossed the lines. Tao told her two sons that management should be strengthened in the system and the employment process should be standardized. If this was not done, there was nothing they could do, even if a traitor appeared.

Someone once asked Tao: "*Laoganma*, you are a billionaire now; why do you still work so hard in the company and do everything by yourself?" Tao didn't have an answer to that question at that point. It kept her thinking all night. Later, she said this at the workers' meeting, "When I leave, I can't take the company with me, and I can't take the Lao Gan Ma brand with me. Then, what am I fighting for? I am fighting for our thousands of employees. I'm working for you all and for our country! I hope everyone will work hard for their own future!"

For more than 20 years, with the help of party committees, governments, and relevant functional departments at all levels, the output value and taxes paid by Lao Gan Ma Company have continued to grow.

Since its establishment in 1996, Lao Gan Ma has developed into the largest pepper product manufacturer in China in terms of production and sales volume. In 2019, sales revenue hit a record high, exceeding five billion *yuan*; in 2020, it hit another record high, exceeding 5.4 billion *yuan*. Lao Gan Ma produces 2.3 million bottles per day and uses 45,000 tons of chili peppers and more than 100,000 tons of rapeseed oil a year.

Today, Lao Gan Ma has built 280,000 *mu* of pollution-free pepper bases in multiple counties in Guizhou, directly and indirectly helping eight million farmers out of poverty. At the same time, it also helps Guizhou Province attract investment and deeply participates in Guizhou's poverty alleviation work through continuous innovation of poverty alleviation ideas.

After she stopped worrying about money, Tao's goal for Lao Gan Ma Company was to become a national enterprise and brand. For more than twenty years, Lao Gan Ma has adhered to the philosophy of prioritizing quality, working hard, and being responsible and practical, as it gradually grew bigger and stronger step by step. The slogan of Lao Gan Ma is to create a national brand for generations to come. Only by developing sustainably and healthily can Lao Gan Ma better support the development of various national undertakings.

Social Responsibility

Paying Taxes
Is Honorable

—Chapter Ten—

Selfless and Candid

Tao was quick-tempered, and people knew it from her argument about taxation; even her swear words were directly quoted in many places.

Tao did everything in accordance with the state policies and never deliberately tried to please anyone. She never escaped one penny of her duty and never allowed anyone to take one penny from her that she shouldn't pay.

When she ran the Shihui Restaurant, an urban management official came to her restaurant on weekends and fined her. He wasn't wearing a uniform and didn't even provide her with a receipt. Tao confronted him, asking him whether he was fining her on behalf of the government or for his private interest. The government did not give him the power to act haphazardly, and he must enforce what should be enforced following required procedures. When he saw that Tao did not conform, the official tried to take away her things, and Tao picked up her spatula and fought him.

Not long after Lao Gan Ma was opened, some people suspected that the company was evading taxes. Tao said, "We always pay taxes proactively and will never evade taxes." After investigating, the tax department found that Lao Gan Ma has paid more than 20 million *yuan* in taxes to the state every year in the past two years, which was convincing enough for a small company like that not to have evaded any taxes.

One evening in the summer of 1998, Tao saw the flood relief operations in the Yangtze River on TV and was touched by the brave police officers and soldiers who fought against the floods with their bodies. Seeing these young men, about the same age as her own sons, standing up in the most critical moment for the sake of the safety of life and property of the people, Tao thought to herself, if she paid more taxes, the state and the people would have more power in overcoming disasters.

Later, the tax department came to carefully check the tax payment status of Lao Gan Ma and made it a model for tax payment publicity. Some people said that *laoganma* was silly in paying all the taxes, while some of which could be exempted or delayed. But Tao doesn't think so. She considered it honorable to pay taxes. "Lao Gan Ma pays taxes honestly and does not do anything illegal. We are grateful to the Party and the government. Our company benefits from the founding of the People's Republic of China, the reform and opening-up policy, our country's entrepreneurial environment changes, as well as the care given by leaders at the provincial and municipal levels. It is this kind of support that made Lao Gan Ma what it is today. Therefore, it is an honor for us entrepreneurs to be able to contribute to the country. The country relies on taxation, and it doesn't matter if we pay more."

One year at the year-end summary meeting, the Tax Department omitted a tax bill of more than 300,000 *yuan*, and Lao Gan Ma's tax bill ranked second in the country. "How did it happen?" Tao got angry on the spot, "Who made this mistake? Where did my 300,000 *yuan* go?" It was a very awkward moment with state leaders and entrepreneurs at all levels present at the conference. The staff of the tax department hurriedly checked and found Tao right. Lao Gan Ma should have ranked first in tax submission with this money. The staff came to Tao and asked if they could settle this in private, but Tao refused. "Absolutely not," she said, "I don't want any bonuses or prizes. You must explain it publicly at the conference. This is your job and your responsibility!"

Laoganma in Real Life

T ao's lack of sophistication often brought her trouble when dealing with the Tax Department. Sometimes, staff with ill intentions would deliberately find trouble with her, but Tao was not someone to be trifled with, either. Despite their rank and position, she was not afraid to confront anyone if needed. But most of the time, compared with many entrepreneurs, Tao was very low-key and rarely accepted interviews because she knew that words caused trouble.

Tao often had to give speeches as an entrepreneur representative of the Nanming District. She wasn't interested in this obligation because she believed her main responsibility lay in managing her company. Therefore, she never spent much time memorizing the speeches written for her but said whatever came to her mind. She knew she could only say the right things when she was doing the right things.

Since she established the company, Tao has been living in the factory. Her bedroom was next to her unadorned office, with a bed, some old clothes, and some old cases she had been using since her wedding day. She has now left the company mainly to her children and does not live there every day like she used to, but she still visits the factory frequently because she likes hearing her employees call her *laoganma*.

Some people asked Tao, "Many private enterprises complain about various taxes, annual inspections, and hidden rules.

Have you ever experienced such pressure when you started the business?" "No," she answered, "I owe no tax to the state, no money to the dealers or employees, and nothing to the customers who trust me and Lao Gan Ma."

Never Ask for Money from the Government

The article "Tao Huabi: Like Wind, Like Fire" in *Foreign Economic and Trade Practice* wrote, "Although she owns a BMW, Tao takes the bus when she occasionally goes to the company so that she is not distanced from her employees. Her sons bought her a villa, but she said it was too far from the company and was unwilling to live there. She likes to live in old houses to hang out with retired employees."

Tao was an exceptional person in many ways. She couldn't read financial statements, but she could memorize them by heart; she didn't know anything about finance, but she could calculate the financial status of the entire company; she also had her unique ways of selecting and hiring talents. After the company grew, Tao felt the need to hire more talented leaders despite the help of her two sons. So, she put up a recruitment advertisement in the local newspaper, and a college graduate, Wang Haifeng, came to the door.

Tao planned to appoint Wang to be the office director, but she did not do so immediately. Instead, she first asked him to do odd jobs in the company and then sent him to various places to carry out anti-counterfeiting tasks, in her words, to "quench him" and "polish him." Half a year later, Tao officially appointed Wang as an office director and, later, an executive in Lao Gan Ma.

Tao took pains in training all of Lao Gan Ma's managers like Wang. As the scale of the enterprise grew and market competition intensified, Tao noticed that some of her "provincial methods" were insufficient. Therefore, she decided to send the company's management personnel to Guangzhou, Shenzhen, Shanghai, and other cities to inspect the market and learn advanced technology from well-known companies. Before leaving, Tao said to them, "I am old-fashioned, but you should not be, and the company should not be old-fashioned!"

The humble, unassuming Tao was a deputy to the National People's Congress, but she was bad at facing the media. One year, when she attended the conference, Tao was surrounded by a group of reporters at the entrance of the Great Hall of the

People. In desperation, she ran away but accidentally got lost. It took the staff a long time to find her.

One year, *Forbes* crowned Tao as the "wealthiest person in Guizhou," which infuriated Tao. Staying low-key about her wealth has become one of her principles, and "not receiving interviews" has become one of her requirements for the management team.

In contrast, Tao was particularly high-profile and fierce on the issue of anti-counterfeiting. According to statistics, there are dozens of copycats and counterfeited Lao Gan Ma products on the market. When Tao was still a deputy to the National People's Congress, she appealed every year to crack down on food fraud and counterfeiting. In addition, Lao Gan Ma spent 20 to 30 million *yuan* in special funds and sent many personnel to search for and crack down on counterfeiting across the country every year. In view of Lao Gan Ma's contribution, the local government awarded Tao special license plates twice.

Tao's success was closely related to her attention to the world around her. Despite her educational background, Tao actively followed national news and learned about political trends. Every important decision she made throughout her career was based on advantageous state policies, such as supportive policies for private enterprises and western development.

In 2000, Tao needed more funds to expand the factory. Some employees told her she could find support from the government on this issue. After the Nanming District Committee of Guiyang learned about her needs, they immediately began coordinating with China Construction Bank to provide a loan to Lao Gan Ma. Tao had never taken out a loan before and did not know about the process. She brought the accountant to the Nanming District Committee and took the elevator to the district head's office. The elevator was very old, and the doors were already broken. When she was leaving, unexpectedly, the doors hooked onto her clothes, causing her to fall. Thinking that it meant borrowing money from the state, Tao said, "You see, the government is also in a difficult situation, and we should not cause more trouble for them." So, they went back to the company.

Do What Her Ability Allows

Judging from Tao's interviews over the years, she had a strong ability to use and control the media. Her principles were: do not receive interviews at insignificant times or on insignificant topics; only receive interviews on important issues or when needing support from public opinions. For example, when the lawsuit was going on with the Hunan Lao Gan Ma, Tao accepted interviews to state her grounds and refuted the rumors set by the other company.

Tao had very clear goals in dealing with the media. Lao Gan Ma was a chili sauce producer, not a celebrity. To her, unfounded accusations against Lao Gan Ma on the Internet were not worth too much of the company's attention to respond since an enterprise's energy was limited. Again, when facing the media on issues related to trademark against the Hunan company, Tao's speech mainly addressed three points: first, the trademark belonged to her according to the law; second, the result she was getting was unfair; third, If the other party won, it would be a blasphemy against the protection of market economic order, contempt for intellectual property rights, and irresponsibility to consumers.

Around 2006, on the 10th anniversary of the company's founding, Tao had an interview with *Contemporary Guizhou* magazine. After that, a large number of articles about her, including "Lao Gan Ma: The Legend from Zero to 100 Million," "Tao Huabi: The Billionaire Boss of Three Characters," and "*Laoganma* Standing on the Starting Line at Age Forty-Two" were released and pushed the reputation of Lao Gan Ma to its peak.

Lao Gan Ma, Wahaha (drinking water), Huawei (mobile phones), and SF Express (delivery service) used to be known as the "unlisted alliance." On July 25, 2018, the Shenzhen Stock Exchange, together with the Guizhou Securities Regulatory Bureau and the Guizhou Provincial Finance Office, investigated Lao Gan Ma, and two other companies participated in a symposium on capital markets serving the real economy. To provide services to enterprises entering the capital market, Guizhou enterprises are welcome to list on the Shenzhen Stock Exchange and issue bonds. Since then, news of "Lao Gan Ma going public" and "Lao Gan Ma entering the listing cultivation period" have been widely spread. In an exclusive interview with Guizhou Radio and Television Station, Tao reiterated that Lao Gan Ma did not consider loans, equity participation, financing, and listing and insisted on doing what her ability allowed. She also said that Lao Gan Ma would never leave Guizhou, the place she was born in and the place she would bring honor to.

News about whether Lao Gan Ma was listed or not was hyped by the media almost every year. In 2018, in particular, the Shenzhen Stock Exchange, Securities Regulatory Department, and the Financial Department simultaneously investigated the company, causing the outside world to mistakenly believe that it was a precursor to Lao Gan Ma's imminent listing. Therefore, one of the purposes of Tao's exclusive interview at that time was to respond to the listing issue that was hotly discussed in society.

Long-Term Layout

Standing at the Commanding Heights of the Industry

—Chapter Eleven—

Preparations for Entering the International Market

C hili pepper was the key to Lao Gan Ma going global and was deeply related to the cultural background of the origin of chili peppers in Guizhou.

As one of the important origin centers of spicy eating customs and widespread cultivation of peppers for more than 400 years, Guizhou had five concentrated distribution areas of chili pepper plantations for cayenne peppers, facing heaven peppers, line peppers and cayenne peppers, line peppers and clustered facing heaven peppers, and facing heaven peppers and mountain peppers.

In the 1960s, peppers from Guizhou Province began to enter the international market, and Suiyang peppers and other peppers were well received in Southeast Asia. China's reform and opening-up policy, as well as the country's economic development in the 1980s, greatly promoted Guizhou's pepper industry. In the 1990s, chili food processing enterprises and chili distribution markets gradually matured, making Guizhou Province the national chili pepper market. As of the first half of 2019, Guizhou's pepper planting area reached over five million *mu*, accounting for about one-sixth of the country and one-tenth of the world.

In recent years, the Guizhou Provincial Government has attached great importance to the pepper industry and regarded it as the province's characteristic, leading industry for poverty alleviation. In 2019, the pepper industry was one of the twelve characteristic industries promoted by provincial leaders.

In order to break down barriers to industrial development, build a platform for communication, exchange, and cooperation among various business entities in the industry, and strengthen information exchange and resource sharing within the industry, the Guizhou Province Chili Industry Association was formally established with the active support of the Provincial Rural Industrial Revolution Group. As a leading figure in the industry, Tao served as the association's honorary president.

The prerequisite for the internationalization of Lao Gan Ma chili pepper oil was product standardization. Tao learned this lesson from her past experience when she was rejected because her products lacked production licenses and standardized packaging. She learned at that time that her products must meet the market-required standards to enter the market.

As various products of Lao Gan Ma became popular in China, some people persuaded Tao, "Your products are so good. You should open up the international market." Tao knew that

China was preparing to join the WTO, which could be a great business opportunity for her company. Therefore, before 2001, the senior management of Lao Gan Ma had already reached a consensus on going international.

Expanding the international market and having the qualifications to enter the international market are two different things. So, Lao Gan Ma had to prepare in advance in order to make the brand bigger and stronger for the international market. Therefore, since 1998, Lao Gan Ma began to send management personnel to Guangzhou, Shenzhen, Shanghai, and other places to inspect the market and gain advanced management experience.

International Style: "Zero Defects"

Tao knew that it was not possible to expand the company with her old methods alone. It was necessary to understand the situations of different cities if the company were to explore the market there.

Lao Gan Ma's products have been rated as "Guiyang Famous Brand Products" by the local government since 1998. The company was also awarded the title of "Advanced Quality Management Enterprise" for its high and stable quality.

The most fundamental things to enter the overseas market are good product quality and meeting the standards of overseas markets. Therefore, Lao Gan Ma had to establish a quality management system and continue to approach the standard of modern enterprises.

Once, at a company meeting, Tao asked about China's entry into the WTO and what benefits it would bring to the company. Others replied that foreign agricultural products could enter the Chinese market in large quantities, and some high-quality agricultural products could be sold at relatively lower prices in the Chinese market due to lower tariffs. In this way, China would not only be able to effectively curb and crack down on criminal activities such as smuggling but also allow the people to enjoy a variety of advanced and convenient foreign goods. After joining the WTO, many high-end consumer goods could enter the homes of ordinary people. For example, the prices of automobiles and telecommunications services would generally fall. People could freely deposit RMB in foreign-funded banks and go to foreign-funded hospitals for better medical services. At the same time, it would be helpful for China to expand exports and enjoy the most favored nation treatment when conducting trade exchanges with member states of the organization, which was going to be a beneficial opportunity for Lao Gan Ma. Tao decided she must not miss it.

"*Laoganma*, you are not truly thinking of selling our chili sauce abroad, are you?" someone asked with great surprise, "The things on TV are not related to us."

"No, they are not," Tao replied, "It is because of China's reform and opening-up that we are what we are today. Entering the WTO is also a measure of this policy, so we must respond to the country's call and go global. What do we need to prepare?"

"To pass some international standard certifications, such as the ISO 9001 international quality management system certification."

Tao learned that repeated inspections were often required during international trade due to different countries' standards. In order to eliminate trade barriers, a set of international standards for quality management was established, namely, the ISO 9001 international quality management system. ISO 9001 was developed with the continuous expansion and increasing internationalization of the commodity economy to improve the credibility of products, reduce repeated inspections, weaken and eliminate technical trade barriers, and safeguard the rights and interests of producers, distributors, users, and consumers.

This third-party certifier was not dominated by the economic interests of both producers and sellers. It was a common standard for quality evaluation and supervision of products and enterprises in various countries. It also served as the basis for customers to audit supplier quality systems.

"Does it mean that certified companies have reached international standards in integrating various management systems?" Tao asked. The management personnel confirmed. "Let's quickly apply, then!" urged Tao.

Around 2000, Lao Gan Ma began to prepare to pass the ISO 9001 international quality management system certification. Some colleagues who were familiar with the international market said, "*Laoganma*, you have always been trustworthy and dedicated to product quality, which is also highly valued in many other countries, so your brand will be very popular abroad." Tao agreed. No one liked to be deceived, and her previous principles would continue to support Lao Gan Ma in its future operations abroad.

Lao Gan Ma immediately started this process and registered with the US Food and Drug Administration (FDA) in 2001. This meant that Lao Gan Ma chili pepper products were exempted from re-certification in most regions and countries around the world. After this, the first batch of chili sauce products was exported to Japan and successfully passed the health inspection by the Japanese Ministry of Health and Welfare. Then, Lao Gan Ma opened up the market in North America, South Korea, France, Australia, New Zealand, Singapore, Thailand, Spain, Ukraine, Bangladesh, Panama, Belgium, and other countries. Tao never expected her original small restaurant and little factory to be known all over the world.

The internationalization procedure of Lao Gan Ma was not always smooth, and issues with patents and trademarks required special attention. For example, when the company entered the German market, the "Lao Gan Ma" trademark had already been registered. So, the company had to engage in patent and trademark wars whenever needed. Other unprecedented challenges arose for Lao Gan Ma to face and tackle. In France, staff worked five days a week, seven hours a day, and their salary was six to seven times that of domestic managers. The company supervisors could not find anyone when they called local colleagues at 5:00 p.m. to discuss the day's work. At first, they thought it was outrageous since Lao Gan Ma managers must stay responsive to work 24/7. However, local employees were needed for communication and for improving work efficiency.

When Tao learned about this, she told the staff in France to be flexible and follow the local people's habits.

Overseas markets were much more complicated than domestic markets for various reasons. Lao Gan Ma remained committed to maintaining its product quality and improving it to meet the standards.

"Wherever Chinese People Live!"

There were many stories about how Lao Gan Ma's popularity abroad, and Tao was always very happy to hear them. Some study-abroad students ate Lao Gan Ma chili sauce at their Christmas party, and those in Switzerland and the UK even established the "Lao Gan Ma Fans Association" on Facebook. An American family also liked Lao Gan Ma chili sauce very much. The husband, Mike, always saved all the peanuts in the chili sauce as the best part for his wife to make her happy.

These stories motivated Tao on her way forward. She felt responsible for defending the reputation of thousands of people in Lao Gan Ma as well as China's national brand.

Lao Gan Ma never deliberately promoted its products, but they have become a necessity for Chinese people when traveling. For many Chinese students studying abroad, Lao Gan Ma provided them with a familiar taste and reminded them of home. People's affection for Lao Gan Ma products made them popular around the world through word of mouth. When asked which countries Lao Gan Ma products were sold to, Tao would proudly say, "Wherever Chinese people live!"

Once, a Guizhou reporter interviewed a first-time traveler from Africa and asked him about his first impression of Guizhou. The traveler said loudly, "Lao Gan Ma." Not many people may know Guiyang Nanming Lao Gan Ma Flavor Food Co., Ltd., but "Lao Gan Ma chili sauce" was a household name in China and was also very popular abroad. Once, an employee showed Tao a newspaper story about someone who went to a country that recently established diplomatic relations with China and saw that Lao Gan Ma was the only "Made in China" product there. Upon inquiry, he learned that Lao Gan Ma in this country was not imported directly from China but purchased from a third country. In China, many people nicknamed Tao the "National Goddess." Some even changed the Statue of Liberty using Photoshop and changed the torch into a Lao Gan Ma chili sauce bottle.

Tao told her two sons and company managers, "We should give ourselves credit for so many people liking our product, but we should also know our responsibility. The more people like us, the bigger our responsibility is."

People asked Tao how she prevented the reputation of her products from falling, and Tao answered, "Quality is the lifeline, and safety is the survival foundation. This is our operating philosophy. Our company always prioritizes product quality and food safety. The first is to ensure the quality of raw materials. Lao Gan Ma has successively built multiple pepper export planting bases across Guizhou, and all export products use soybean oil. For other raw materials, the qualifications of suppliers are strictly reviewed, and packaging materials are strictly inspected."

Tao always said governmental support had been crucial to Lao Gan Ma's export process from the aspects of information, technology, scientific research, standards, etc., so that the company could further improve the market access filings in developed countries and regions in Europe and the United States, including US FDA filings, Japanese Ministry of Health and Welfare annual inspections, and Korean Health Department Product Testing, etc. With outstanding product quality, Lao Gan Ma has expanded overseas markets in more than 50 countries and regions. In 2011, Lao Gan Ma exported 1,412 tons of products and earned $5 million in foreign exchange, making it the largest private enterprise in Guizhou in terms of foreign exchange earnings at that time.

In 2005, as the market expanded, Lao Gan Ma's production capacity became seriously insufficient. The company relied on technicians with more than ten years of work experience in proportioning ingredients, frying, filling techniques, etc. It took a long time to train such a technician, and it was impossible for Lao Gan Ma to achieve a win-win situation in terms of quality and output in a short period if it continued to follow the traditional manual production model. So, the company decided to make technological transformation and innovation the top priority for enterprise development.

People also asked, "*Laoganma*, you already made so much money; why do you still want to expand foreign markets?"

Tao answered, "Lao Gan Ma has indeed made a lot of money over the years, but my thoughts are simple. I feel sad that many people abroad cannot access my chili sauce, and I want to change that."

Therefore, Tao concentrated her employees and funds on implementing three technological transformations and innovations to improve efficiency through automated production. From 2006 to 2008, Lao Gan Ma invested 100 million *yuan* to implement the first phase of technical transformation, completing the semi-automatic gas wok frying process for export products, semi-automatic filling, automatic jar cleaning, disinfection, drying machines, ingredients proportioning, workshops and large comprehensive warehouses and other projects. In 2009, another 290 million *yuan* was spent on full automation, and projects such as mechanized capping, automatic labeling, automatic carton sealing, palletizing, de-palletizing, and automatic frying machines were completed. Now, the company was moving toward full intelligent production.

After Lao Gan Ma achieved production and management standardization, it could quickly meet market demand at any time. It was a challenging process, and Tao needed to cope with many new concepts and possibilities, for example, to trust machines to master the proportion of ingredients, the heat of frying, and the filling skills. She remained suspicious about the change and only allowed the system to be put into operation after repeated experiments, and the product's taste was similar to what she had made.

With the outbreak of the international financial crisis, consumption levels in overseas markets continued to decline, and many countries implemented suppressive policies on imported products. Since 2007, domestic food safety incidents have occurred frequently, making food safety a hot topic of concern. The development of food production companies has become increasingly difficult under these dual influences.

Do One Thing and Do It Well

To help Lao Gan Ma meet international standards and open up foreign markets, the Guizhou Entry-Exit Inspection and Quarantine Bureau increased its support by adding corresponding regulatory procedures to protect Lao Gan Ma's export sales and efficiency.

In 2008, Lao Gan Ma was sanctioned by the European Union for unqualified sealing gaskets. Lao Gan Ma relied heavily on foreign trade companies and had little control of overseas markets. Facing a series of problems, Tao reflected, "We should not be afraid of problems. The key is to actively solve them. We will do what we can, and the market will push us to do better. We implement in accordance with international standards, which will better promote our products to the world."

Since 2009, Tao has appointed her eldest son, Li Guishan, to take charge of overseas markets. Authorized agents from importing countries and regions were selected, and various regulatory systems, such as an agent deposit system, quality tracking system, safety guarantee system, monthly assessment system, and market expansion monthly report system, were established and implemented. These allowed Lao Gan Ma to continuously formulate and adjust its market expansion plan in line with local needs in a timely manner and to have a relatively concentrated number of buyers when it directly connected with overseas customers. Understanding and following relevant policies and measures of the importing country in time, the Guizhou Entry-Exit Inspection and Quarantine Bureau provided Lao Gan Ma with the most direct channel to improve its production process and achieve a win-win for the company and its import agents.

Expanding the overseas markets raised various challenges, including complex and strict food export procedures, brand infringement, product quality improvement, food safety guarantees, etc. Although the sales share in the foreign market could not compete against the sales volume of any domestic province, and sales costs and risks were much higher, considering the needs of international students and overseas Chinese markets as well as the enterprise's long-term development, Tao persisted down this path. Tao's principle was to prioritize overseas orders with ensured quality and safety. However, no matter how hard she tried, problems still occurred.

One day, when she arrived at her office, Tao received news that some products had been returned from Australia. According to the spokesperson for the New South Wales Food Safety Authority, the packaging of Lao Gan Ma chili sauce did not indicate that it contained peanuts, which may cause people with peanut allergies to consume it by accident. There were 480 bottles of chili sauce involved in the case, each weighing 270 grams. The loss was not big, but it had a huge impact. Some people began to suspect whether Lao Gan Ma had quality issues. Tao did not respond to the doubting voices because she believed time could explain everything. Later, the Guizhou Entry-Exit Inspection and Quarantine Bureau responded to the recall initiated by the Australian company Tek Shing Trading Pty Ltd. It turned out that these products were abnormal export products and not from Lao Gan Ma. On the English labels attached, the peanut was artificially removed from the ingredient during translation. The Tek was also not an authorized seller of Lao Gan Ma. Therefore, this batch of products was not inspected by the bureau and did not have corresponding inspection and customs clearance certificates.

In those years, Lao Gan Ma's abnormally exported products that had not been inspected by the bureau were recalled four times. Due to differences in domestic and foreign standards, diets, and technical barriers to foreign trade with China, products sold abroad through unofficial channels could easily be notified. "In recent years, Guizhou's export volume of specialty products such as cigarettes, wine, tea, and peppers have increased significantly. However, due to abnormal exports, unauthorized sales, and quality issues, recall incidents reported by foreign officials have left serious negative impacts on the company and Guizhou's food exports."

With other departments and the company itself, the Entry-Exit Bureau severely cracked down on abnormal export products in order to protect Guizhou enterprises overseas effectively. In addition, The bureau strengthened and transformed technical trade measures into an important basis for export supervision. By making full use of these measures on the domestic market, it helped export enterprises improve product quality.

Despite the continuously arising problems, Lao Gan Ma's reputation abroad remained unchallenged. When her employees felt concerned about the recall incident in Australia, Tao stayed confident and positive about the trust the company had built with its customers based on its integrity and product quality.

Due to various factors such as tariffs, dealers, and costs, Lao Gan Ma changed its "low-price strategy" in the foreign market and took a high-end route. Some people also suggested adjusting the products for foreign tastes, to which Tao answered, "Our core competitiveness is our products. As long as we persist in making good products, everyone will like them."

Luxury from a Small Workshop

In 2013, Gilt[*] described Lao Gan Ma products as "noble condiments," making it equivalent to 70 to 80 *yuan* per bottle with a limited-time sale price. When asked about her opinion,

---

[*] An online shopping and lifestyle website based in the United States.

Tao said, "Our products are indeed much cheaper in China than abroad. As a Chinese person, I feel proud that my products are selling well in other countries."

After more than ten years of hard work, Lao Gan Ma successfully passed the inspection by the US FDA at the end of 2014. In early December of that year, the US FDA officially approved Lao Gan Ma as the first export food manufacturer in Guizhou to enter the US market.

Now, Lao Gan Ma has become the leading enterprise in the chili industry in China. Its products occupy more than 60% of the domestic market and are exported to many countries and regions, such as the EU, the US, Canada, Japan, Australia, and New Zealand. Guizhou has also become China's largest producer of processed chili peppers and plays a pivotal role in the national chili industry.

Keeping Pace with the Times

The Inevitable Brand Rejuvenation

—Chapter Twelve—

Reject Listing

In 2014, Lao Gan Ma was selected as one of China's top 500 most valuable brands, ranking number 151, with a brand value of 16.059 billion *yuan*. In 2016, Lao Gan Ma's average daily production capacity reached three million bottles, exported to 72 countries and regions, and achieved a tax revenue of 700 million *yuan*. It was selected as one of the leading enterprises in Guizhou's "Thousand Enterprises Transformation" project.

As Tao got older, Lao Gan Ma was gradually taken over by her sons, Li Guishan and Li Hui. Tao only held 1% of the company's shares, and she only participated in some major company affairs. Her two sons held 49% and 50%, respectively. Many were not optimistic about family businesses and believed that the leadership position of the elderly in family businesses was critical. In their eyes, family businesses were exclusive, patriarchal, rigid, and difficult to be carried on by spendthrift children. Tao was well aware of these disadvantages, but she insisted on making Lao Gan Ma a family business, believing it to be the only way for Lao Gan Ma to succeed. If an enterprise wants to grow, everyone must work together toward the same goal, just like the example of Li Ka-shing's company or many other family businesses in

Western countries. "Family business" and "modern business management mechanisms" were not contradictory terms, and it was
with modern enterprise management systems that family businesses could grow faster and bigger.

After graduating from high school, Guishan joined the
army and then worked in the 206 Geological Engineering Team.
As his mother's chili pepper business grew, Guishan offered to
help. With her son, Tao could say whatever she wanted without
concern or restriction, so Guishan's participation in the company
was a great relief for her. She appointed him her first general
manager and intentionally trained both her sons to be familiar
with all production procedures. When Guishan first came to the
company, Tao sent him to the factory, where he learned to cut the
pepper roots, wash, smash, and fry the peppers, and understand
how to control the humidity, warmth, and time during production.
When Hui joined the company, Lao Gan Ma was already well-
developed, but Tao still sent him to the front line. After working
in the company's finance department, Hui obtained a license to
be a senior economist.

Later, Guishan expanded overseas markets and stayed
abroad all year round. The two brothers took full responsibility

for the company, with Guishan in charge of sales and Hui in charge of production. When it came to areas that neither of them could deal with, they would seek help from others.

At the same time, Lao Gan Ma did not exclude talented people from taking important positions and often planned learning trips for them. Tao kept learning, too. She tried her best to learn financial-related knowledge so that she would not be deceived about the company's matters. When her employees increased, she also learned architecture so that the company could provide them with a comfortable dorm building. Her design, which Guishan made fun of at first, was eventually implemented.

Lao Gan Ma achieved an annual sales revenue of 3.72 billion *yuan* in 2013 and a paid tax of 510 million *yuan*. Many people then persuaded her to go public, including leaders of government departments and investors in the market. According to them, going public could help family businesses achieve rapid financing at a low cost, reduce their dependence on banks, reduce their debt ratio, and improve their credit ratings. In addition, it could help family businesses achieve leapfrog development with standardized management and financial systems.

At that time, Tao knew nothing about going public, so she asked for everyone's advice and found that many outstanding entrepreneurs were very conservative and cautious. Later, Tao responded, "You don't need to persuade me anymore. I am determined not to go public. It is deceiving other people's money with our current performance. I won't do it."

Many listed companies would do anything for sales and to attract investment. But Lao Gan Ma was different. Tao never lied about the company's performance and only strived for what her ability allowed. After her previous experience as a vegetable vendor, she always insisted on paying and delivering goods on the spot so that she didn't owe anything to her employees and suppliers, and the suppliers wouldn't owe anything to her.

Many institutions in Beijing and Shanghai came to Tao to discuss listing, but she felt this was a waste of time. Aside from frying chili peppers, which she was good at, she didn't want to know anything about raising funds or operating capital.

A Beijing company came to Lao Gan Ma with the Guiyang government personnel to discuss its listing issues. However, the company's administrative department rejected them based on Tao's principles of "no loans, no financing, and no listing." Two other companies had come before but were also rejected.

Tao was firmly against loans. A seemingly large business empire could collapse in an instant because it had grown beyond its capabilities. Having a sound business strategy was much better than a blind expansion to keep the risks within control. Tao insisted on doing everything within her capacity and never even applied for government-subsidized loans. Over-reliance on government support would cause the enterprise to lose motivation, and complete reliance on bank loans would cause it to become dependent on funds. A company would be drained by financing institutions little by little, eventually leading to bankruptcy. Tao taught her sons never to buy shares, never hold shares, never go public, and never take loans. These four things must be guaranteed to ensure that her children and grandchildren could carry on her heritage.

Lao Gan Ma's structure was designed based on efficiency. The company did not have a board of directors, vice chairman, or deputy general manager, but only a financial management department, a marketing department, a general department, a production plant department, and a corporate management affairs department. The managers all worked hard on the front line, and they were required not to accept any interviews. "Running a business is not being a celebrity. We do not need to be on TV or in newspapers all the time. We need to focus our time and energy on our jobs," said Tao.

Tao couldn't read and knew nothing about finance, but she could memorize her company's financial statements by heart after someone read them to her. She never used a calculator, but she could tell if there were any problems with the numbers. Many people thought she was born with such talents, but her skills in memorizing and fast calculation were developed during her days selling vegetables on the street.

The advantage of family businesses is that they are not as rigid as others, such as state-owned enterprises. Lao Gan Ma provided employees with flexible working hours based on their job categories and needs. At the same time, Lao Gan Ma adhered to the rules such as "don't be lazy" and its requirement for employees' work efficiency as well as prioritized social responsibility for its long-term development.

The Mysterious Shareholder Li Miaoxing

In January 2017, news about Tao withdrawing her shares came out, and a mysterious man named Li Miaoxing owned 51% of Lao Gan Ma's shares. Based on the Industrial and Commercial Department's website, Li Guishan held 49% of the shares, Li Miaoxing held 51%, and Tao's name had been deleted. The investor's information regarding Guiyang Nanming Chunmei Brewing Co., Ltd., another company owned by Lao Gan Ma, also changed in 2014, with Li Miaoxing becoming its sole shareholder with a total investment of 15 million *yuan*.

Since Lao Gan Ma rarely interacted with the media, everyone was curious about this mysterious shareholder, Li Miaoxing. Some people found that Li Hui was serving as the vice chairman of the CPPCC of Nanming District in Guiyang City and was in charge of contacting the non-public economy according to work needs. He was also the president of Lao Gan Ma.

Some self-media reported, "Li Miaoxing, who owns 51% of the shares of Lao Gan Ma, has very little public information and is said to be a family member." Others found from the National Intellectual Property Administration website that since 2010, three out of thirty-seven patents of Lao Gan Ma were owned by Li Miaoxing. They analyzed that, judging from how Li Miaoxing controlled or invested in Lao Gan Ma and its subsidiaries, he was probably an insider of the company, which was famous for its family management model. On the 2017 Hurun rankings,*

---

* The Hurun Report is a research institution based in China that is known for its lists of the rich and rankings of the wealthiest individuals in China and globally. The reports cover various aspects of wealth, including the richest individuals, companies, and other related rankings.

Tao was not on the list. Still, Li Miaoxing and Li Guishan both ranked among the top ten richest people in Guizhou, with wealth values of 3.8 billion *yuan* and 3.7 billion *yuan*, respectively. Their joint wealth totaled 7.5 billion *yuan*, which was Tao's wealth value of the previous year.

As the number of calls for verification increased, Tao explained that "Li Miaoxing" was Li Hui's former name.

Due to health reasons and aging, Tao missed the Two Sessions in 2016 and 2017, and her cervical problems caused by long-term standing and lifting of weights deteriorated. This was why she decided to let her sons take over the company and continue her career for her. Today, Lao Gan Ma has three production plants located in Guizhou, with a total area of 750 *mu* and nearly 5,000 employees. Every day, Lao Gan Ma provides a variety of delicious and healthy products to more than two million consumers.

Starting to Use the Big Data Platform

In 2016, with the guidance and support of the Nanming District Government, Lao Gan Ma invested nearly seven million *yuan* in tailoring a set of operational big data platforms to optimize control and management of raw material procurement, product production, and finished product sales through six models, including the sales monitoring, most popular products analysis, dealers' analysis, raw material price monitoring (early warning of natural disasters in origin), etc.

Compared with using phone calls to monitor market conditions in the past, big data monitor solves the problem of delayed feedback and can accurately place goods on the market. Based on the real-time monitoring data of the operational big data supervision platform, Lao Gan Ma adjusts its product marketing strategy with customer needs as the core, achieving seamless integration of production and sales and precise product launch so that there is a sufficient supply of popular products and no backlog of other products.

Not long ago, based on market demand, Lao Gan Ma introduced two new products: the vegetable oil hot pot base and the spicy hot pot base. According to the dealers' analysis, vegetable oil hot pot base was more popular in the northern market, but the quota was insufficient, while in the southwestern market, there was an excess quota. The opposite was true for the spicy hot pot base. Therefore, the company promptly adjusted the sales and quota plans of the two regions and reduced some products to supplement them in the opposite market. Now, the sales of the two products are growing by more than 10% every month.

The raw materials required for the production of chili sauce include chili peppers, rapeseed oil, Sichuan peppercorn, soybeans, etc. The procurement and reservation of these raw materials are directly related to the company's cost control, profit margin, and production stability. It was difficult for market researchers alone to understand the rapidly changing market conditions in the past, but the "raw material price monitoring (natural disasters in origin)" early warning module platform has effectively solved this problem.

In June 2018, hail occurred in major pepper production areas such as Gansu and Sichuan. The "raw material price monitoring (original natural disaster early warning)" module issued an early warning during the trial operation. The company immediately made predictions, adjusted its procurement strategy, and ensured a safe stock of the peppercorns. After the Lao Gan Ma big data supervision platform was launched, the company achieved annual cost savings of 15% to 20% on average through monitoring, early warning, and early processing of raw and auxiliary material procurement, as well as accurate calculation of manual use.

Interdisciplinary Development

Now that the company is managed by young people, Lao Gan Ma has been upgraded in people's eyes. Tao doesn't know what big data is. She only knows that this platform can receive consumer data and feedback in a timely manner, and the company can make corresponding market adjustments based on this feedback.

Through the data compiled by the "most popular product analysis" module, Lao Gan Ma can comprehensively analyze consumers' tastes in each sales area and guide the development of new products based on public taste. At the same time, after the new product is launched, the company can rely on this module to adjust and optimize the product according to consumer feedback, thus effectively enhancing the product's market adaptability and ensuring that every new product is well received.

On September 18, 2018, the Tmall flagship store online of Lao Gan Ma released a "99 bottles of Lao Gan Ma + OC customized sweatshirt" package priced at 1,288 *yuan*, which was sold out as soon as it was put on the shelves. This sweatshirt was first unveiled at the 2019 Spring and Summer New York Fashion Week "China Day." The sweatshirt collaborated by Lao Gan Ma and Opening Ceremony instantly attracted the world's attention. It was bright red, the same color as the Lao Gan Ma chili sauce packaging, with the characters *laoganma* and Tao's profile printed in the middle.

Tao said she could no longer keep up with the thinking of young people, but she supported their new ideas and hoped they would never stop creating new things. People's love for life and pursuit of delicious food provide endless motivation for Lao Gan Ma to strive for customers' long-term satisfaction and recognition.

As always, Lao Gan Ma insists on quality first. Every chili pepper and soybean used in its product is carefully selected. To create a taste that meets market demand, Lao Gan Ma purchases chili peppers from all over the country and tests different proportions consisting of peppers from different regions, varieties, tastes, and colors, creating the most satisfying and recognized products for the whole country and the world.

Lao Gan Ma
over the Years

—Appendix—

1998   ✳ Awarded the title of "Advanced Taxpayer" by
     Nanming District.
     ✳ Awarded the title of "Advanced Major Taxpayer" by
     the Nanming District Local Taxation Bureau.
     ✳ The series of products were rated as "Guiyang Famous
     Brand Products" by the Guiyang Municipal People's
     Government.
     ✳ Awarded the title of "Advanced Quality Management
     Enterprise" by the Guiyang Municipal People's
     Government.
     ✳ Awarded the "Advanced Enterprise in Implementing
     Technical Supervision Regulations" by Guiyang
     Municipal Bureau of Technical Supervision.
     ✳ The product "Lao Gan Ma Flavored Soybean" was
     rated as "Guizhou Province Famous Brand Product."

1999   ✳ The product "Lao Gan Ma Flavored Chili Sauce" was
     rated as a "Guiyang City (Recommended) Famous
     Brand Product."
     ✳ The product "Lao Gan Ma Flavored Chili Sauce" was
     rated as a "Guizhou Province Famous Brand Product."
     ✳ Rated as "Top Ten Private Enterprises in Guiyang
     City" by the Guiyang Municipal Committee of
     the Communist Party of China and the Guiyang
     Municipal People's Government.
     ✳ Rated as "Advanced Economic Work Unit" by
     Nanming District.
     ✳ Rated as "Top Ten Taxpayer Enterprises" by Nanming
     District.
     ✳ "Tao Huabi's Lao Gan Ma trademark" was rated as
     "Guizhou Province Famous Trademark."
     ✳ Awarded the title of "National Quality and Efficiency
     Advanced Enterprise" by the China National Food
     Industry Association.

2000 ❋ Rated as "Key Enterprise in Nanming District, Guiyang
City."
❋ Rated as "Guiyang City's Advanced Private Enterprise in the
Non-public Economy."
❋ Awarded the title of "Guizhou Province Non-public
Economy 'Star Enterprise'" and "1999 Township Enterprise
Development 'Advanced Enterprise'" by the Guizhou
Provincial Committee of the Communist Party of China and
the Guizhou Provincial People's Government.
❋ The product "Lao Gan Ma Fresh Minced Beef" was rated as a
"Guizhou Province Famous Brand Product."
❋ Rated as "National Advanced Unit for Quality Management
of Township Enterprises" by the Ministry of Agriculture.

2001 ❋ Awarded the title of "Advanced Unit for Party Building
Civilization" by the Guiyang Municipal People's Government.
❋ Won the title of "Top Ten Large Taxpayers."
❋ Rated as "Key Leading Enterprise in Agricultural
Industrialization Management in Guizhou Province" by the
Guizhou Provincial Department of Agriculture and eleven
other departments and bureaus.
❋ Named one of the "Top 20 Leading Food Enterprises in
China's Agricultural Industrialization Management" by the
China National Food Industry Association.
❋ The series of products was rated as "2001 China International
Agricultural Expo Famous Brand Products."

2002 ❋ Jointly rated as an "Integrity Taxpayer Enterprise" by the
Guizhou Provincial State Taxation Bureau and the Local
Taxation Bureau.
❋ Awarded the title of "Advanced Party Building Unit for
Non-public Industrial Enterprises" by the Guiyang Municipal
People's Government.
❋ Awarded the title of "Civilized Unit of the Year 1999–2002"
by the Guizhou Provincial Committee of the Communist

Party of China and the Guizhou Provincial People's
Government.

* Rated as "Advanced Unit for the Development of Township
  Enterprises" by the Guizhou Provincial Committee of the
  Communist Party of China and the Guizhou Provincial
  People's Government.
* The annual tax payment ranked fifth among Chinese
  private enterprises in the ranking list compiled by the State
  Administration of Taxation.
* Passed ISO 9001 international quality management system
  certification.

2003 * Awarded the title of "Advanced Unit in Party Building
        Civilization" by the Guiyang Municipal People's
        Government.
* Honored as one of the "Top Ten Large Taxpayers."
* Rated as one of the "Top Ten Star Enterprises" by the
  Guiyang Municipal Committee of the Communist Party of
  China and the Guiyang Municipal People's Government
* Became the exclusive sponsor of the Guizhou Quality and
  Integrity Enterprise Alliance.
* Named as the "Outstanding Enterprise in the Food
  Industry of Guizhou Province."
* The registered trademark "Lao Gan Ma" was rated as a
  "Famous Brand in the Food Industry of Guizhou Province."
* Awarded the title of "Enterprise with Outstanding
  Contribution to Tax Payment" by the Nanming District
  Committee of the Communist Party of China and the
  Nanming District People's Government.
* Awarded the title of "Advanced Party Building Unit
  for Non-public Industrial Enterprises" by the Guiyang
  Municipal People's Government.
* The annual tax payment ranks tenth among Chinese
  private enterprises in the ranking list compiled by the State
  Administration of Taxation.

2004 ✽ The product "Chili Sauce" was evaluated as "Green Food."

✽ Rated as a double-excellent brand with "assured quality and user satisfaction" by the China Foundation of Consumer Protection.

✽ The products "Fresh Shredded Pork with Soybeans" and "Red Oil Fermented Bean Curd" won the third prize and encouragement award for Guiyang City's Outstanding New Products.

✽ Won the title of "2003 Key Non-public Economic Advantage Enterprise."

✽ The registered trademark "Lao Gan Ma" was rated as "Top Ten Famous Trademarks in Guizhou" and "Consumers' Favorite Brand" by the Guizhou Provincial Administration for Industry and Commerce.

✽ Recognized as a "National Key Leading Enterprise in Agricultural Industrialization" by eight ministries and commissions, including the Ministry of Agriculture, National Development and Reform Commission, and Ministry of Finance.

✽ Awarded the title of "National Food Safety Demonstration Unit" by the Organizing Committee of the China Food Safety Annual Conference.

✽ Jointly rated as an "A-Level Tax Credit Enterprise" by the Guizhou Provincial State Taxation Bureau and the Local Taxation Bureau.

✽ The annual tax payment ranked 25th among Chinese private enterprises in the ranking list compiled by the State Administration of Taxation.

✽ Passed ISO 14001 environmental management system certification.

2005 ✽ Awarded the title of "The First 50 Integrity Units in Guizhou Province."

✽ Awarded the title of "Demonstration Unit for Managing Factory According to Law."

✳ Awarded the title of "Guizhou Province Intellectual Property Pilot Unit."

✳ Recognized as a "National Key Leading Enterprise in Agricultural Industrialization" by eight ministries and commissions, including the Ministry of Agriculture, National Development and Reform Commission, and Ministry of Finance.

✳ Awarded the "Best Achievements Award" for products exhibited at previous China Food Expos.

✳ The products "Fresh Shredded Pork with Soybeans," "Spicy Crispy," "Spicy Chops," and "Spicy Chicken" were rated as "Guiyang City (Recommended) Famous Brand Products."

✳ Named "National Agricultural Product Processing Demonstration Enterprise" by the Ministry of Agriculture.

✳ Jointly rated as an "A-Level Tax Credit Enterprise" by the Guizhou Provincial State Taxation Bureau and the Local Taxation Bureau.

✳ The annual tax payment ranked 37th among Chinese private enterprises in the ranking list compiled by the State Administration of Taxation.

2006 ✳ Passed Hazard Analysis and Critical Control Point (HACCP) certification.

✳ The series of products won the Excellence Award in the 2006 "Kailin Cup" Colorful Guizhou Tourism Product "Two Competitions and One Meeting" Guiyang City Selection Tourism Product Design Competition.

✳ The series of products won the Special Nomination Award in the 2006 "Kailin Cup" Colorful Guizhou Tourism Product Design Competition.

✳ Won the title of "China Famous Brand Product."

✳ Won the title of "2005–2006 National Outstanding Leading Food Enterprise in the Food Industry."

2007 ✳ "Tao Huabi Lao Gan Ma and Pictures" won the title of "Well-Known Trademark."

2014 ✳ Ranked 151st in the list of "The Top 500 Most Valuable Brands in China in 2014" with a brand value of 16.059 billion *yuan*.

2017 ✳ The company's operating income was 4.549 billion *yuan*, and the tax payment was 755 million *yuan*, ranking second among the top 100 private enterprises in Guizhou, second only to a real estate developer in Guiyang with 834 million *yuan*.

2018 ✳ China's brand value evaluation information was released, and the company ranked second among food processing companies with a brand value of 12.148 billion *yuan*.

2019 ✳ The company's sales revenue exceeded five billion *yuan*, setting another record high. The annual sales revenue was 5.02251 billion *yuan*, a year-on-year increase of 14.43%; the tax paid was 636 million *yuan*, a year-on-year increase of 16.82%.

2020 ✳ The annual sales revenue was 5.40009 billion *yuan*, an increase of more than 300 million *yuan* over 2019 and a year-on-year increase of 7%.

Bibliography

Bu, Yi. *The Legendary Lao Gan Ma*. Beijing: China Yanshi Press, 2013.

Li, Qichen. *Laoganma Tao Huabi's Wisdom in Management*. Beijing: New World Press, 2015.

Li, Yun'e. *Yunguan Village and the Story of Lao Gan Ma*. Guiyang: Guizhou People's Publishing House, 2001.

Liu, Hairong. "Lao Gan Ma Settling in Guiyang." *China Business Herald News Weekly*, June 10, 2003.

Xiao, Lu. "Tao Huabi: Three Firsts, Four Wishes," *Contemporary Guizhou*, no. 24 (2006): 14.

Zhan, Yongfa, Zhou Guangping, Tian Yingshu, et al. "Research on the History of Chili Pepper Cultivation in Guizhou Province and Its Main Types and Distribution." *Beijing Agriculture*, no. 27 (2015): 35–39.

Zhang, Lina. *Lao Gan Ma's Founder Tao Huabi: I Will Starve If I Am Not Tough*. Beijing: Sino-Culture Press, 2016.

Zhang, Rui. "Tao Huabi: Like Wind, Like Fire." *Foreign Economic and Trade Practice*, no. 9 (2015): 12–16.

Zhou, Xibing. *The Spicy Legends of Lao Gan Ma*. Guangzhou: Guangdong Economy Publishing House, 2016.

About the Author

Wu Hua, a seasoned media professional, scriptwriter, and author, has dedicated his career to in-depth reporting and storytelling. With a rich background as a chief journalist, magazine editor-in-chief, and deputy editor, Wu Hua has left an indelible mark on journalism. His notable works in in-depth reporting include "The Price of Slaughter," "In Search of the Tiger," and "Lama's Wealth Creation Chronicle," earning him multiple accolades such as the Guizhou Provincial Journalism Award and the prestigious first prize in the national metropolitan daily *Evening News* Good News Awards. In addition to his journalistic achievements, Wu Hua is a published novelist with works like *Yi's Bandit King Mai Wang* and *Shadow Horse*. His novel *Shadow Horse* was honored with the inaugural Guizhou Provincial Literary Award for Best Novel in 2022.